The Character-Based Leader

Instigating a Leadership Revolution . . .
One Person at a Time

Lead Change Group, Inc.

This edition published by

Dog Ear Publishing

4010 W. 86th Street, Ste H

Indianapolis, IN 46268

www.dogearpublishing.net

ISBN: 978-145751-222-3

This book is printed on acid-free paper.

Printed in the United States of America

Praise for The Character-Based Leader

Woven through the pages of this book is a clear, sorely needed message: "Personal Character is the foundation of genuine leadership." This book applies equally to leadership in a business setting as well as to leading ourselves, our families and our communities. I encourage you to read, learn, apply and teach these principles to others.

~ Mark Oakes

> Chief Executive Officer / Owner of Intellimar, Inc., Concentric Security, LLC and Blue Ember Technologies, LLC

This is a fantastic collection of current, relevant and timely leadership insights! The contributors have put forth stories and lessons that can be put into action immediately. It's definitely needed, especially now. I encourage you to purchase the book, and invite a group of friends and colleagues to go through it together. I assure you the experience and outcomes will be as powerful for you as it will be for your team and organization.

~ Laura Goodrich (@LauraGoodrich)

> Author of *Seeing Red Cars*

The perspectives in this book further the dialogue on effective leadership at a time when the human experience is undergoing unprecedented global changes.

~ Heath Harding, PhD

> Associate Director, Illinois Leadership Center, University of Illinois

This wonderful collection of 21 different perspectives on leadership is a treasure trove of delight. If you value diversity of opinion, well thought-through analysis and actionable teaching – or if you just want to keep up with leading edge thinking on what leadership truly is, then buy this book.

~ Les McKeown

> Author of the WSJ bestseller *Predictable Success*. His second book *The Synergist: How to Lead Your Team to Predictable Success* has just been released.

If you want to learn about and be encouraged about Character-Based Leadership, you've come to the right place. Take 21 smart people writing about an important topic, and what you get is this book. Read these pages, knowing you will find ideas that will help you make a bigger positive difference in the world around you.

~ Kevin Eikenberry

Author of the bestselling books, *Remarkable Leadership* and *From Bud to Boss*

The Character-Based Leader presents a comprehensive perspective on how to be the authentic leader you already are. It's not a prescriptive set of generic behaviors – it's a model for examining yourself and defining your own personal character, values and leadership using practical and applicable tools. The breadth of leadership perspectives, ideas and approaches shared by the authors will help leaders in all walks of life grow into the Character-Based Leaders they aspire to be.

~ Mike Figliuolo

Author of *One Piece of Paper: The Simple Approach to Powerful, Personal Leadership*

The *Character-Based Leader* is an inspirational quilt of leadership stories, research, examples, advice and wisdom from some of the most influential voices in social media. Reading each chapter was like eating chocolate chip cookies – I couldn't stop myself until the entire plate was finished. This book reads like a virtual dialog, with diverse, intelligent and provocative perspectives on the complex leadership characteristics of trust, integrity, respect, humility and perseverance. If you're serious about leadership, and you're ready to make a real commitment to change, then I'd highly recommend reading *The Character-Based Leader*.

~ Dan McCarthy

Writer of the award-winning leadership development blog "Great Leadership," and Director of Executive Development Programs at the Whittemore School of Business, University of New Hampshire

Some leaders feel pressured to choose between focusing on the people or on the bottom line. Success lies in inspiring and engaging people to reach beyond the bottom line. As new and experienced leaders reach out to tap the secrets of engaging others, this book guides all to first reach within to bring Character-Based Leadership to life. A worthy read.

~ Kate Nasser

The People-Skills Coach™

This is a great leadership guide from a volunteer group of 21 authors who tell us how to use their experiences, best practices, mistakes and core values to become Character-Based Leaders.

~ Kristine Scotto

Principal at The Primrose Group Consulting

INVALUABLE! *The Character-Based Leader* is a rich collection of ideas from some of the best thinkers around.

~ Frank Sonnenberg

Author of *Managing with a Conscience*

In our dramatically-evolving world, yesterday's leadership characteristics serve to create the very gravity that weighs down our organizations. *The Character-Based Leader: Instigating a Leadership Revolution...One Person at a Time* is a must read for any leader who wants to step forward into 21st century opportunities, approaches and thinking.

~ Rebel Brown

Author, speaker, business strategist and executive coach

The definition of effective leadership is in the midst of a long-needed and profound change, from "nuts and bolts" and "dos and don'ts" to something more deeply personal and human. The Lead Change Group are among the change agents leading the charge in their online and offline communities, and they combine forces to give this new definition added weight and traction in their new book, *The Character-Based Leader.*

Words and concepts (that certainly sing to me) like "trust" and "integrity" and "humility" are among the building blocks in the book that are explored and expanded upon by this group of authors, in this well-presented volume. These 21 writers have provided vivid proof via this excellent book that the best ambition of their collective vision of Character-Based Leadership is to selflessly build something great that cannot be built alone.

~ **Terry "Starbucker" St. Marie**

Managing Partner, Inside-Out Thinking/SOBCon

Edgar Puryear, the reigning expert on military leadership, says that character "is everything in leadership." The authors of this book would agree. They've put together a rich collection of thoughts on the kind of Character-Based Leadership that makes a difference. If you're concerned about the quality of leadership in our whitewater world, you should read this book. If you help develop leaders, put it at the top of your must-read list.

~ **Wally Bock**

Author of *Performance Talk*, writer of "The Three Star Leadership" blog

We have seen the devastating effects resulting from the drift away from Character-Based Leadership. Our character is manifested in our leadership. *The Character-Based Leader* effectively places the need for character development front and center. It inspires us to go deep within and discover who we are and who we need to be in order to lead effectively. In this collection of essays by seasoned leaders, you will rediscover the meaning and expectations of true leadership. They remind us that the content of our character will determine the content of our leadership.

~ **Michael McKinney**

President of LeadershipNow.com

Wow! I would have liked to have read *The Character-Based Leader* about thirty years ago, before I started my military career. It provides a step-by-step guide to being a leader of character that would have been invaluable to my development within my chosen profession.

   ~ Scott J. Farrell

      U.S. Army, Retired, and owner of Positively Speaking

The Character-Based Leader is a must-read for anyone who seeks to understand – and master – the nearly-lost art of genuine leadership. Within the pages of this short, quick read, twenty-one leaders from a variety of fields come together to spell out their audacious prescription for a better world through better – more genuine, more sincere, more sustainable – leadership. There is a better way to lead. Reading *The Character-Based Leader* will help any leader discover that way and instigate that change for herself, the LeadChange way. I couldn't put it down. You won't, either!

   ~ Ted Coiné

      Author of *Five Star Customer Service* and *Spoil 'Em Rotten!*, and co-founder of SwitchandShift.com

To fulfill the potential our future offers, we desperately need character-based leaders. Now 21 passionate authors have combined their talents to deliver a cohesive message that is both inspiring and informative. Peppered with stories and examples, *The Character-Based Leader* is about making a choice. Read it and be ready to take action!

   ~ Jesse Lyn Stoner, Ph.D.

      Co-author with Ken Blanchard of *Full Steam Ahead! Unleash the Power of Vision*

Table of Contents

Table of Contents

Table of Contents

Acknowledgements

To those who travelled from around the country to begin the conversation about Character-Based Leadership in person for the first live Lead Change Group event, Leaderpalooza. Thank you for taking a leap of faith to invest a weekend with people you barely knew and never met. Your continued commitment, collaboration and friendship are gifts I treasure: Deb Costello, Monica Diaz, Sonia DiMaulo, Vicky Henry, Jim Holland, Steve Keating, Fanny Korman, Susan Mazza, Mark Oakes, Jane Perdue, Erin Schreyer, Don Shapiro, David Wachs and Chris Zaucha.

To Shawn Murphy for getting this project started. We wish you could have been part of the book and want you to know how much we all appreciate your commitment, time and effort to create its framework and launch us in the right direction.

To the 21 authors who invested their time, talents and wisdom to make this book possible. I am deeply honored by your commitment and contribution to bringing the Character-Based Leadership revolution to life in the pages of this book.

To the countless people who have given us their time and support throughout the book writing, publishing and promotion. A special thanks to Becky Robinson, Kevin Eikenberry, Mike Myatt and Angie Chaplin.

To the entire Lead Change Community for all the energy and wisdom you contribute to the Character-Based Leadership revolution in all you do and the many ways you contribute to the conversation.

To our editors Tara Alemany, Deb Costello and Don Shapiro for accomplishing the amazing task of weaving the work of 21 different authors into one cohesive voice. Your commitment to excellence shines through in the finished project. A special thanks to Tara Alemany for leading the editing team and for taking personal responsibility in so many ways for ensuring we delivered a book we can all be proud of.

To those authors who gave your time and talents in support of editing, publishing and promotion, thank you for all the ways you

Acknowledgements

stepped up to lead and do what was needed: Heather Coleman-Voss, Sonia DiMaulo, Georgia Feiste, Chery Gegelman, Christina Haxton, Will Lukang, Susan Mazza, Jennifer Miller, Jane Perdue and Lisa Petrilli.

To all of those who supported the authors in making this book possible. Among the 21 authors there are many spouses, significant others, children, mentors and friends who gave us the support and freedom to invest ourselves in writing this book. We are truly grateful for your support and your faith in us.

To everyone who has the courage to lead from who you are. You inspire us as you help write the story of Character-Based Leadership and instigate the revolution where you live and work.

~ **Mike Henry Sr.**
Founder, Lead Change Group
April 2012

One Voice on Character and Leadership from 21 Authors

There are books written by a single author and there are anthologies, which represent a collection of authors' works on a common topic. The book you are holding in your hands is neither of these.

The Lead Change Group chose to do things differently. This all-volunteer, non-profit group found 21 members who wanted to contribute to a book that delivered a consistent message through their individual styles, focus and expertise.

Some chapters touch on very general themes. Others go into great detail. Some are about the overall issue of character and leadership. Others present specific "how-to" suggestions that can help readers implement the book's ideas. Some may come across as academic, while others share very personal stories. Although there may be differences in the details, all the authors agree on the core message of this book; that *character counts in leadership, and there are key elements that shape character.*

This book has been written through a collaborative and consensus-building process that mirrors the core beliefs of members of the Lead Change Group. While no one was in charge, everyone was involved, acting as both a leader and a follower at the appropriate times.

Each author's chapter was reviewed by an Editorial Committee who focused on how the chapter supported the book's theme and the vision of the Lead Change Group. Authors were asked to tweak portions of their chapters so they would all support common themes about Character-Based Leadership.

Enjoy the diversity of styles and specifics covered in this book while remembering its core message. We need a leadership revolution so that character becomes the top priority in evaluating and developing leaders. Making character count in leadership is the change that the Lead Change Group hopes you will help instigate. You *can* make a difference.

Part I

Why Character-Based Leadership?

Chapter 1

Instigating a Character-Based Leadership Revolution

Chapter 2

Why Character-Based Leadership?

Chapter 3

A Crisis of Character

Chapter 4

Make the Most of Your Human Resources

Chapter 1

Instigating a Character-Based Leadership Revolution

Mike Henry Sr.

The term "Character-Based Leadership," as used by the authors, rose out of a desire to capture the idea of leadership being espoused by a group of leaders in social media and Internet channels in the summer and fall of 2009. The group had been formed in late March of 2009 with an initial mission of "applying leadership to make a positive difference." As the members of this social community began to interact more, the term *Character-Based Leadership* began to surface.

In a series of conference calls, we adopted the term Character-Based Leadership to characterize the type of leadership we commonly shared, but even then

> *Character-Based Leadership is leading from who you are rather than from your power or position.*

members of the group had trouble defining it. The group's mission became "applying Character-Based Leadership to make a positive difference."

Initially, some members felt that we should direct our efforts at defining character by creating a list of core traits. Others thought the focus should be more on a central common definition avoiding the creation of another list of character traits, so throughout the winter of 2009, we all attempted to define Character-Based Leadership with a simple definition. Finally, after considering the many things Character-Based Leadership was not, we decided that it was leading from who you are, rather than from your position or power. Character-Based Leadership is not a particular style of leadership or a key set of behaviors. Rather, it is, to paraphrase Mark Oakes, making the decision that you *are* a leader. Instead of simply deciding to run a triathlon, a greater transformation occurs when you decide to become a triathlete. At that point, your actions emanate from who you are. Character-Based Leadership is not a list of behaviors, but is about who you are at your core.

Once that definition was decided and articulated, however, the problem wasn't solved. Fifteen of us met at LeaderPalooza 2010 in Ft. Lauderdale, Florida, and a number of other things became quickly apparent in our relationship. First, we each agreed that we see a movement taking place. People aren't satisfied with where they are and where leaders are. We trust leaders less than ever. Many of the generation entering the workforce do not aspire to become leaders.

We have a crisis of leadership and a need to personally be involved in changing the world of leadership for the better. It's not that we feel leadership development is the problem, but rather that the current methods aren't keeping pace with the need expressed by individuals. In a way, individuals in the world are in search of leadership help faster and in a greater variety than it is being provided. We wanted to be a part of the revolution that we were experiencing. In fact, as Susan Mazza eloquently stated, we wanted to take part in *instigating* this revolution.

Instigating a Leadership Revolution

Second, we all agreed that Character-Based Leadership is needed, and we were (and are) excited to advance the idea. However we each used different words, feelings and descriptive concepts to voice our thoughts. Each of us describes Character-Based Leadership differently, and yet we agree. Even in writing this book, we balance a desire to maintain the individuality of the authors while creating a cohesive message that resonates. When we each bring the best of who we are to the practice of leadership, we find that each person's character varies the definition. Snowflakes share characteristics but they say no two are exactly alike. No two people are exactly alike. Therefore, no two people will live the definition of a Character-Based Leader the same.

This is our attempt to connect you with your own inner passion to live your life as the change you believe the world needs.

Underlying Principles

You will see three core underlying principles running through the descriptions in the following chapters:

1. Leadership is influence.
2. Influence is given.
3. People give influence based on competence, trust and purpose.

Each principle forms the foundation of what you're about to read.

Leadership Is Influence

John Maxwell has quite famously stated, "Leadership is influence, plain and simple." It is the ability to get someone else to want to do what you want them to do. Leadership respects the individual and their choice to contribute.

Influence Is Given

Simon Sinek has stated that we can only inspire or manipulate. Every individual in the developed world is a free agent (even though we acknowledge that many people around the world are not free). Degrees of freedom may be applied, but everyone is free to choose whom they support, what they support, and the degree to which they support an idea. Seth Godin calls this "emotional labor" in his book *Linchpin*, quoting Arlie Hochschild. We choose the degree to which we bring our creative energies to an effort. We choose the degree to which we innovate, excite, mobilize and serve others. In the end, cooperation with a leader is contributed.

People Give Influence Based on Competence, Trust and Purpose

Competence. First, we want to know if the leader can get us to the group's objective. Although I might trust my wife to want me to be well, I don't always take her medical advice and I would never let her operate on me. We must believe that the person we choose to join has the ability to get us to the objective.

Trust. Second, we must believe that the leader will get us to our objective. In addition to reaching the group's objective, we need to know the leader will do so in a way that doesn't violate our best interests, but helps us achieve the benefit we expect from joining the effort. We want our leaders to be *for us*, not simply for themselves.

Purpose. Finally, we must believe the purpose is worth the effort. We may believe the leader capable and we may believe the leader to be trustworthy, but the leader may have a vision and direction contrary to where we want to go. Without regard to the quality of the purpose, we simply must have an aligned purpose or we won't give the leader much influence or authority over us. We will withdraw our cooperation if the leader's objectives and ours begin to separate.

Now you understand a bit of the history and the foundation for the remainder of the book. This book isn't designed to be instructional, but rather inspirational. We hope to excite you about the idea that your personal leadership makes a critical difference in the world. We want to challenge you to bring the best *you* to the marketplace of ideas and to make a positive difference. We want you to achieve your greatest accomplishments based on who you are. Remember, great accomplishments are those that benefit others. Bring your best self, your true character, to make the greatest difference for people in your sphere of influence. That's Character-Based Leadership.

Chapter 2

Why Character-Based Leadership?

Chery Gegelman

*The world is crying out for leaders who build up,
nurture and enhance; rather than tear down exploit
and dominate.* ~ **Laurie Beth Jones**

When I first started using social media, I sent out a lot of quotes like the one above and quickly learned that the quotes that consistently received the largest number of responses were the ones that touched on a source of pain and a need for change in our workplaces and in our society.

Recently, fellow Lead Change contributing author, Tristan Bishop, reminded me about the television show *Undercover Boss*. I found myself pondering how much that show resonates with the public and the reasons that it is so popular.

Would you rather work with someone who:

- Won't take the time to define what they want, but consistently growls like a grizzly and berates people for doing the wrong things or for taking no initiative?
- Cares more for their people and the mission than for themselves?
- Helps to develop your greatest strengths and empowers you to make a difference?
- When faced with a crisis, is so focused on finding someone to blame, they have no ability to problem solve?
- Provides a motivating vision, removes obstacles, and celebrates you, your work and the impact you are making?

- Has a great vision and desire to serve, then gets distracted by their own success?
- Means what they say, says what they mean, and apologizes when they make mistakes?

Consider the number of leadership speakers, authors, and bloggers whose content is continually devoured by the public. Do you see the emphasis on our human quest for something more?

In all of these examples, there is a common theme that people want to be valued, to be understood, and to be given the opportunity to make a difference. Would it surprise you to realize that our leadership needs today are the same as they were thousands of years ago? They have been spoken in slightly different words at different times and through different people, but the truths themselves are the same. Take a look:

Love your neighbor as yourself.
*~ **Jesus Christ***

A leader is not an administrator who loves to run others, but someone who carries water for his people so they can get on with their jobs.
*~ **Robert Townsend***

People don't care how much you know until they know how much you care.
*~ **Theodore Roosevelt***

Life's most persistent and urgent question is, "What are you doing for others?"
*~ **Martin Luther King Jr.***

Leaders provide for their people what the people cannot provide for themselves.
*~ **John Maxwell***

The purpose of influence is to speak up for those who have no influence.
*~ **Rick Warren***

So why does history keep repeating itself? Perhaps it is to emphasize lessons that have already been learned. Maybe it's to humble us into the realization that modern society is not much more sophisticated than ancient society. Maybe it is to encourage us with the knowledge that Character-Based Leadership is not a new concept and it is not difficult to understand or to apply. It is just a series of simple truths that have been time-tested and continually proven.

Or maybe it's because, as humans, we naturally believe that the world should revolve around us. For many of us, it has taken a life-altering circumstance or a season of brokenness before we understood that life and leadership really is not about me. That lesson becomes our defining moment and causes us not just to be willing to bend our knees and serve others, but also to actually desire those opportunities. We begin to realize that each time we serve others from the deepest parts of our hearts, we are filled with intense compassion and new insights.

If you are a titled leader, seeking to lead differently, be encouraged. You don't have to drive over people to achieve results. You can choose to be a Character-Based Leader while unleashing greatness in each individual and throughout the organization. When you choose this path, it will be much like setting up a computer for the first time. The initial investment of time and energy is greater than what you may be currently doing. However, in the long run, you will create a more efficient and less stressful workplace for everyone (you included).

- First, find someone who is willing to hold you accountable for your actions and behaviors.
- Then, focus everyone on a shared vision and purpose.
- Finally, dig deep to uncover the gifts of each individual on your team, and focus yourself on serving and developing the individuals and the team as a whole.

By doing so, you will begin to inspire confidence, expectation and hope in those you lead, and as the team develops you will experience increasing momentum and, eventually, a flood of uncommon results.

If you are not a titled leader, but you share this vision, you may be wondering how to create a case for change that will be heard and responded to by those in titled leadership positions. Begin by applying one of Stephen Covey's *Seven Habits*, "Seek first to understand, then to be understood." Understand that people don't know what they don't know and that, like children, titled leaders have learned what they have lived.

- Those who have been abused frequently become abusers.

- Those who have lived in fear create fear-based environments.
- Those who have worked in environments without integrity frequently create environments without integrity.
- Those who have been told not to think but just to do expect the same from others.

The book of Proverbs says that without a vision, people perish. Sharing a vision with titled leaders will require courage and commitment, but consider this: If you can't or won't, who will? And if no one does, how can change be created? And if no one steps forward to lead change, what will the effect be on future generations?

*It always seems impossible until it's done. ~ **Nelson Mandela***

Chapter 3

A Crisis of Character

Don Shapiro

Consider three individuals who stepped up to the plate as leaders when no one asked them and they didn't have to:

Kizzy, a single mother in Milwaukee, watched the evening news about a mob of teenagers ransacking a convenience store only to see her 13-year-old daughter and 15-year-old son on the store's video footage. The next morning she gathered her kids and took them to the police station. She said to the officers, "If you don't bring them in, you are telling them it's okay." Two other parents turned in their kids, but parents of the other 15 teenagers have yet to come forward.

Allan Guei recently graduated from Compton High School. As a star basketball player, he received a full scholarship to college. A month before graduation, Allan competed in a basketball free throw contest that offered a $40,000 first prize to pay for college. Allan won the contest, but at his graduation ceremony he gave the $40,000 to seven other players who had competed in the same tournament, keeping nothing for himself. He said he already had a scholarship and these other athletes who were struggling financially needed the help to go to college.

A distributor of bicycles and parts had a great warehouse manager named George and an able assistant named Jesus. Sometimes both George and Jesus had to leave the warehouse to attend management meetings or to handle special problems. After they left, things would start to unravel amongst the warehouse crew. Coordination between pickers, inspectors and packers broke down. But only for a short while, because every single time George and Jesus left, Skip, one of the warehouse workers, would fill the leadership void. Soon, the warehouse was humming along as if George and Jesus had never left. No one asked him to do this. George never said anything to the crew about Skip assuming this role. Skip just stepped up to the plate and made it happen every single time.

At home, in the community, and at work, every day we are presented with choices that offer the potential for us to step up and lead if only for a moment. Too often, when we think about a leader, we imagine someone with a title or position that puts them in charge of others. A title such as supervisor, manager, coach, director, president, minister, teacher or parent does not make someone a leader, however, and people without any titles or positions are acting as leaders when it really counts... in that moment when leadership can make the difference.

So it has come to pass that some people with or without titles successfully swing the leadership bat every day while others, faced with the same choices, either don't do anything or do the wrong thing, harming themselves, those who have followed them, and the organizations they belong to. For every Kizzy, Allan and Skip, there are far too many individuals who don't do the right thing. Lately, too many of those who have chosen the wrong path have become national or international news. Their lack of leadership and poor choices have harmed tens of millions of people personally and financially.

A Puzzling Contradiction

This leaves us with a puzzling contradiction. During the past 30 years, a focus on leadership has turned into a growth industry. Books, training, development programs, groups, discussions and mentions of leadership have grown exponentially. Entering the word "leader" into a Google search during July 2011 produced close to a billion results, while entering the term "leadership" produced 94,600,000 results. Literally, anything that anyone wanted to know about leadership appears to be easily available and, more importantly, it seems like almost everyone has had some exposure to the idea that good leadership is needed.

How can so many still be falling short as leaders with this much emphasis on leadership? Clearly, there is more to being a good leader than well-documented techniques, methods and practices. Leadership isn't simply a skill or a body of knowledge that one memorizes. Leadership isn't about a person being given an important title and people simply following that person by virtue of their title. The increasing incidence of bad leadership in families, schools, charitable organizations, churches, research labs, associations, corporations and government cries out for a solution. As this book will explore, the leadership crisis is really a crisis of character. And that crisis is getting worse by the day.

The crisis may appear to be about leaders who are publicly visible, but this crisis isn't just about people in high positions. What's important to realize here is that individuals who have attained a position of importance come from all of us. Fathers, mothers, cousins, community volunteers, members of congregations, friends, and more are all thrust into leadership roles whether they wanted those roles or not, and those who arrive at positions of importance started from the same place as the rest of us.

The crisis is in people's character, not in the positions that people attain. If Kizzy, Allan and Skip move into positions of importance, the character they have already demonstrated will be there to guide them. They will

> *To produce a world of great leaders at home, in the community, and in organizations, the time has come to make people's character priority number one.*

continue to do the right thing because it's the right thing to do, regardless of what positions they hold personally or professionally. Where did that character come from? How did they know to act the way they did? Why are there too many individuals who lack this kind of character, and what can we do about it? To produce a world of great leaders at home, in the community, and in organizations, the time has come to make people's character priority number one.

How Bad Is the Crisis?

First, it's important to understand just how bad the problem really is. Although most people are aware of a few individuals in positions of power who have displayed a lack of character and can cite the damage they have perpetrated, this problem is much more pervasive than most people realize. Calling it an epidemic might be considered a stretch, yet there is no question that lack of character, bad leadership and questionable choices are rising at an alarming rate in all areas of society.

Government

Issues of character involving those in the government go beyond the headlines. When you Google "misconduct by government," it produces 13,700,000 results, and "abuse of public trust by elected officials" produces 1,270,000 results. Thousands of web pages are filled with news articles from every US state that talk about city, county and state elected officials along with school boards and other elected bodies all reporting violations of the public trust. As an example, Citizens Union, a watchdog group for the state of New York that tracks abuses of power, made the following report:

> During the past six years from 2005–2010, 13 legislators left office because of criminal charges or ethical misconduct—more than triple the four legislators who left during the previous six-year period from 1999–2004.

If the pace of bad leadership and lack of character tripled in the New York State Legislature just in the last six years, what is the chance that the same escalation is happening elsewhere? But this problem is not just about elected officials who make the evening news. Ethics Resource Center's 2007 National Government Ethics Survey reported the following conclusions about those who work for the government at all levels:

> Nearly six in ten government employees saw at least one form of misconduct in the past twelve months. The strength of ethical culture in government workplaces is declining, while pressure to commit misconduct is growing. 30 percent of misconduct across government goes unreported to management.

The problem of poor choices and lack of character is with people at all levels, not just with those who hold titles and positions of importance.

Military

A May 21, 2011, article in the *Army Times* reports the results of a survey that shows the effects of bad leadership on soldiers in the Army.

> Poor leadership is driving soldiers to leave the Army. The results come from a survey by the Army Research Institute that showed 26 percent of sergeants and staff sergeants and 23 percent of lieutenants and captains surveyed planned to leave the Army after completing their current service obligations.

> Of those, 35 percent of enlisted and 26 percent of officers cited the quality of leadership at their duty stations as a reason for leaving. Poor leadership was the top reason selected by the active-duty enlisted survey participants and the third-most popular reason among the active-duty officers surveyed. Among noncommissioned officers, leadership concerns were a greater motivation to quit than the relentless pace of deployments....

This is disheartening news coming from an institution that is critical to both national and world security. As the report concluded, much of the blame for this trend in the Army and possibly other branches of the military comes from promoting too many too fast without proper evaluation and training.

Medical Doctors

Medical doctors are considered one of the most respected professions, yet the incidence of violations of ethics, misconduct and more appear to be higher than what one would expect from a profession that goes by the Hippocratic Oath to do no harm. A Google search for "misconduct by doctors" will produce 4,260,000 results. "Doctors losing their medical license" returns 33,600,000 results, though there is significant duplication due to stories that have gone viral.

When duplicates from any of these results are eliminated, it still leaves an astounding number of cases in which doctors made bad judgments and displayed bad leadership. One of the most troubling examples is of a doctor who headed an endoscopy center in Las Vegas.

Dipak Desai was a gastroenterologist who ran the Endoscopy Center of Southern Nevada. He faces racketeering, insurance fraud and neglect charges related to a hepatitis outbreak that authorities believe infected at least seven, and as many as 114 patients. The outbreak was caused because Dr. Desai ordered everyone working in the center to reuse syringes for anesthetics to save money, which contaminated the vials of anesthetics. He was a real life "horrible boss," and many have suffered because he failed to do what he promised to do when he became a doctor.

Corporations

Since the recession, corporations have been under a microscope, with significant blame leveled at Wall Street and companies in the finance, banking and insurance sector. But questionable decisions are not limited to events during the recession or to those at the top. A Google search for "violations of public trust by corporate executives" produced 15,700,000 results such as these two:

Hewlett-Packard CEO Mark Hurd resigned for submitting false expense reports concerning his relationship with a contractor.

David Sokol, rumored to be Warren Buffett's successor, was forced to resign for trading in Lubrizol stock prior to recommending that Berkshire Hathaway purchase the company.

If someone at the top does these things, what type of message does that send to everyone else, from those working for them to kids watching the news? This leads to the question as to why corporate management can go down the wrong path.

As Novartis chairman Daniel Vasella told *Fortune* magazine:

...for many of us the idea of being a successful manager—leading the company from peak to peak, delivering the goods quarter by quarter—is an intoxicating one. It is a pattern of celebration leading to belief, leading to distortion. When you achieve good results... you are typically celebrated, and you begin to believe that the figure at the center of all that champagne-toasting is yourself.

The problem in business is not limited to those in positions of authority, however. The 2009 National Business Ethics Survey, conducted by the Ethics Resource Center, reported that 49% of employees say they have witnessed misconduct and 38% of firms still lack ethical cultures. Most troubling was the increase in retaliation against employees who reported misconduct. Some of that was by other employees at the same level, not just by superiors.

Clergy, Teachers, Parents and More

While the Catholic Priest molestation scandal may be the most well known among religious misconduct, it turns out that violations of the trust that congregations place in the clergy occur in every religion. A Google search of "misconduct by religions" produces 13,500,000 results, while "misconduct by ministers" yields 5,420,000.

A search for "misconduct by teachers" produces 3,890,000 results on Google, and "misconduct by parents," 6,360,000. Yes, most teachers, parents and members of the clergy are good people doing their best for their students, families and congregations. But the number of bad apples is simply too high. Every poor choice is an act of leadership in the wrong direction because it can lead others to do the same thing.

In Search of Character

All these violations of trust come down to people making bad choices. This isn't about skills or techniques or methods. It's a crisis of choice. Everyone will face choices that affect other people and organizations. Some of those choices deal with questions of right and wrong. Others are about the willingness to address a problem instead of ignoring it. And many choices are simply about speaking up instead of doing nothing. For every error of commission, there are many times more errors of omission... simply saying and doing nothing when a situation cries out for just a little leadership.

Misconduct, violations of ethics, and bad decisions by those in positions of authority is only one part of the problem. Clearly, these same things are being done by people who do not have authority, as has been reported by government and business ethics surveys. The rising reports of child neglect, overzealous parents at youth sporting events, and cheating on exams are but a few examples that show how crisis in character touches every part of our society.

This all comes down to a crisis of character. There are simply too many people in all walks of life and at all levels of authority who are not acting with character. Character starts at home, in school, and through religious institutions. If we are seeing a lapse of character at these levels, is it any wonder that children are growing into adults who lack enough character to become Character-Based Leaders?

Kizzy, Allan and Skip are Character-Based Leaders. They lead from who they are, not because of any title or position. In spite of the leadership crisis, more people are actually like Kizzy, Allan and Skip than not. People of good character are everywhere. This crisis doesn't require people in positions of power and importance to solve it. Everyday people, you and I and the neighbors across the way, can all decide the time has come to make character priority number one. And when we do, we will lead an effort that will change the world.

It Starts at a Young Age

Clearly, the starting point to build a society, a country, a world filled with Character-Based Leaders is in the home. It starts with what every parent says and does every day. Yes, parenting is tough. It's demanding. It can be too easy for a parent to give up on the drill and just let kids do what they want. Today's parents are stressed out and pressed for time. Staying on top of what their children do and not letting anything pass that could be a lesson about character isn't easy.

Every time a parent cheats or takes advantage of something and their kids witness it, they are broadcasting a role model that says it's okay to do these things. When parents let their kids get away with something because they don't want them to get in trouble with the school or the law, they have lost a good opportunity to teach their children accountability and personal responsibility. If parents fail to consistently communicate what is right and wrong because they don't want any more drama at home, they are walking away from their role as leaders and developers of the leaders of tomorrow. These are all choices that result in bad leadership.

The leadership role in the home, at school, and in the community begins the second we make it a top priority. When we think it's important to lead, we will. When we believe that leading from good character is critical, we will apply that to ourselves and to those closest to us. So the first step is for every parent to realize they are in a leadership role and that everything they do broadcasts a lesson about character. The same goes for teachers, school administrators, members of clergy, and community volunteers.

The Leadership Bell Tolls for Thee

Almost daily, situations that cry out for a little leadership happen right in front of us. They happen in the home, at stores, on the street, at a parent-teacher conference, during a youth soccer match, in church, on Facebook or Twitter, at work, and in thousands of other instances. In that moment, what do you do? What do you say? What will your actions or inactions say to others? Yes, you have the power to make a big difference. Everyone every day can step up to the Character-Based Leadership plate like Kizzy, Allan and Skip did. When enough of us do that day in and day out, it will communicate a model for others to follow. When we lead through our own character, we help shape the character of those around us.

We all have to take some responsibility for the lapses of character we see displayed on the TV, on the internet, and in front of us. Each lapse of character didn't just happen. It is the result of certain foundations not being embedded during childhood. Such lapses continue into adulthood when no one speaks up and offers good feedback to those who display a lack of character. Whether from parents, schools or community organizations, somewhere along the line these people didn't learn what character means. They were not guided to develop the strength to do the right thing even when there's pressure to do otherwise.

When everyone of good character draws a line and says that character counts all the time in all places, the revolution begins. To do that means we cannot remain quiet when we see someone sending a child the wrong message or when we see an adult making a choice that displays a lack of character. If you see a friend of yours doing that, do you remain silent because you don't want to upset them? Or do you speak up? When we are in a situation where our actions and words will send a message to others, what choice will we make?

Situations that cry out for us to lead happen in an instant and may not be easy to address. Yet, with a little strength backed by good character, we can make a difference. When tens of millions of people every day say that good character is priority number one, things will begin to change for the better.

We need a lot more leaders like Kizzy, Allan and Skip. We need everyone to step up to the plate and to lead from positions of character regardless of who they are, where they are, or what they're doing. This is how we solve the leadership crisis, because leadership isn't about one's title or position… it's about who we are inside. Leadership is all about character.

We all have to take some responsibility for the lapses of character we see…

No single book, including this one, can offer all the answers. It is the hope of the Lead Change Group and all those who volunteered to collaborate on this effort that, by shining a spotlight on the heart of the issue, we might ignite a revolution. If enough people who seriously care about the future can, through their own efforts and explorations, put more focus on character itself… who we are as people and how we develop that in others… we can start a revolution that changes our world for the better.

Chapter 4

Make the Most of Your Human Resources

Mary C. Schaefer

The relationship between leaders in Corporate America and employees today has me concerned. It's as if a number of leaders in top positions have lost track of the *very distinctive value* that their human resources bring, to make their businesses prosper. If we are to capitalize on the unique value of human beings at work, the fundamental relationship between people who are employees and those who endeavor to lead them must change. Those relationships must be stable and respectful, supported by leaders making decisions based on sound principles versus shortsighted reactivity.

To be clear, when I use the term "leader" here, I'm talking about executives at the top who are making decisions in the name of the company. Their decisions affect not only stockholders, but also the livelihoods of potentially thousands of people who are employed by them, most of whom they will never look in the eye.

The American work culture has gone through plenty of change since the industrial revolution. In the past 25 years particularly, financial pressures have compelled corporate leaders to make decisions like outsourcing, off-shoring and downsizing. Add to the mix benefits reductions, budget cuts, pay freezes, and mandatory unpaid time off, and it's no wonder that more than 70% of US workers are reported as "disengaged," according to Gallup's "State of the Global Workforce, 2011."

Though the intent of these actions was to create financial stability, inside some company cultures, it felt like employers were moving away from taking care of employees to expecting employees to manage their own careers and create their own job security. This is not without merit, but the shift from one perspective to the other does not seem to have been facilitated. Employees and their managers need to actively transition such changes in a constructive way to resume engagement.

Granted, the financial environment over the past few decades has been unprecedented as the global economy emerged. Who *would* know what to do in the face of continual financial challenges? But isn't that a leader's responsibility?

Let's look at the case of downsizing decisions specifically. In the past 25 to 30 years, leaders have chosen downsizing as a routine response, often repeatedly at the same company. Yet, studies by Harvard Business School, the Census of Manufacturers, and Wayne Cascio, author of *Responsible Restructuring*, overwhelmingly show that downsizing does not improve stock price, immediately or over time. Among these studies, it is also shown that downsizing does not improve profitability or productivity, nor is it a reliable way to cut costs.

What's going on here? Are leaders not looking at the data? They are looking at some data, or they would not be compelled to make decisions to lay off in this instance. But clearly that is not the whole picture.

In exploring the case of downsizing, we find it is shown to be as much a response to what others are doing (i.e., imitation) as it is to financial need, according to Arthur Budros, Associate Professor of Sociology at McMaster University in California. Jeffery Pfeffer, a professor in Stanford's Graduate School of Business, goes so far as to assert in a *Newsweek* article from February 2010 that some companies now cut jobs to minimize hits to profits, not to ensure the company's survival.

An American Management survey finds that 88% of companies that had chosen downsizing reported that morale declined. I don't have an MBA or any experience in the executive suite, but who among us could not anticipate an ultimate negative impact on human beings repeatedly exposed to decisions that leave them feeling irrelevant and disposable?

This is a disappointing state of affairs, to say the least. I'm not saying that downsizing is never the right response. But what are we left to conclude when company leaders continue to make decisions that do not improve their companies' viability and that create a disengaged workforce?

What are the alternatives for companies facing financial difficulties? Let's look at corporate leaders' decisions in the context of downsizing by looking at the airline industry immediately after 9/11. All US airlines, except one, did what other corporations had been doing for years, immediately instituting layoffs of tens of thousands of people. For one company, it seems that its leaders remained grounded in the belief that their employees' knowledge and skills are invaluable, and they made decisions to preserve and grow that investment.

At this date, that one exception, Southwest Airlines, still has not had an involuntary layoff during its 40 years. It was ranked fourth in Fortune's World's Most Admired Company list for 2011 and was also the largest domestic carrier by total passengers in 2010. As a former head of human resources for Southwest told Stanford Professor Jeffrey Pfeffer, "If people are your most important assets, why would you get rid of them?"

What I would like to see today is more corporate leaders really thinking through the effects of their decisions on their workforce, and not simply making these high-impact decisions out of imitation or habit. Corporate leaders undoubtedly have access to the same research we do about employee disengagement and the ineffectiveness of downsizing, but some leaders continue to take action that damages the talent they already have available at their fingertips. Somehow, Southwest leaders see a way to maintain financial stability and even increase profitability without creating a disinterested workforce.

Southwest's type of leadership requires character and the principles of integrity and responsibility that go along with it. Only through Character-Based Leadership will leaders make decisions that preserve the ability of their human resources to thrive and to deliver results beyond expectation. The more that human beings at work are engaged by all of what makes us human, the more our organizations will benefit by the results that only committed and motivated human beings can create.

Being human means having very human needs, such as the need to contribute, to be appreciated, to make a difference, and to belong. Human needs can be viewed as a weakness or simply as underutilized traits that can be taken advantage of, allowing both employees and companies to profit. These needs must be addressed in every decision and every interaction. Leaders can adapt to this approach by learning to take everyone's needs seriously, even if they don't understand or relate to those needs.

Ultimately, an engaged workforce is best for all stakeholders, including customers, society, employees and stockholders. By trading on the power of relationships, we will see employees creating ideas seemingly out of nowhere or accomplishing the impossible. When all involved see the express benefit of their relationships and of individuals' roles and contributions, our organizations will experience the true competitive advantage of their human resources.

The act of adhering to principles can be challenging in the face of industry norms, the momentum of large organizations, or the current overwhelming "leadership by position" perspective. It takes the stamina and strong foundation of Character-Based Leadership to swim against the tide.

My wish is that, one day, we will all be lifted by the inestimable power and potential in human beings at work treating each other like human beings. Our society will grow and prosper in a whole new way because employees will do their work knowing that they play an essential role and truly make a difference.

If corporate leaders are to capitalize on their greatest asset, they must rediscover the importance of fundamental relationships between human beings. I can't tell you exactly what this will mean for your decisions and actions as leaders. I'm asking you to truly look at your employees with a more character-based approach, with an eye to what human beings can bring to the table and gain from it. This commitment to taking responsibility to honor each other's worth, and the way life itself is expressed through the productivity of people's heads, hands, or hearts; it is not only a decision, but also a journey. I hope that through your struggles to see this vision in action, you realize its power.

Part II

Lead from Where You Are

Chapter 5

Leading with Character by Leading from Within

Chapter 6

Leading from Our Strengths

Chapter 7

Using Your Head to Manage and Your Heart to Lead

Chapter 8

The Choices We Make

Chapter 5

Leading with Character by Leading from Within

Lisa Petrilli

There is no escaping the fact that when we show up for work and for our leadership roles, we bring the entirety of ourselves to the table. We bring our convictions, our strengths, our fears, and our weaknesses, along with our insecurities, knowledge of our past failures, pride in our past accomplishments, and our desire to lead our teams successfully.

> *To be a leader of true character involves understanding who you are, within yourself, at your deepest and most personal level.*

I believe that to be a leader of true character requires a connection with, and acceptance of, our whole selves. I also believe that being a leader of true character requires not only a vision of where you are taking the organization you are leading, but also a clear personal vision that clarifies why you're working with and leading that organization in the first place. **It involves understanding who you are, within yourself, at your deepest and most personal level.**

Only by being truly connected with ourselves at every level, by facing this truth, and by having a personal vision can we come into our roles as leaders and say to our followers (in essence), "This is who I am, what I believe, where I am heading, and why I am heading in that direction. Please put your faith and trust in me, and please follow me down this path."

By sharing this vision with our followers and *letting our leadership flow from within,* our followers can:

- Hold us accountable and expect actions to match our words.
- Understand our character, from which we will lead.

"Leading from within" is a topic I am passionate about, and one that I believe represents a lifelong journey.

It's my honor and pleasure to share with you three leaders whom I believe are excellent examples of what it looks like to exude Character-Based Leadership that comes from within.

Abraham Lincoln

I have found Lincoln to be a most inspiring form of visionary, one who creates his vision from a reverent respect for the past and values that exude from within him and that are essential to his very being.

In his book *Lincoln on Leadership,* Donald T. Phillips says:

It's well known and documented that during the Civil War Abraham Lincoln, through his speeches, writings, and conversations, "preached a vision" of America that has never been equaled in the course of American history.

Lincoln provided exactly what the country needed at that precise moment in time: a clear, concise statement of the direction of the nation and justification for the Union's drastic action in forcing civil war....

His vision was simple.... It was patriotic, reverent, filled with integrity, values and high ideals. And most importantly, it struck a chord with the American people.

It was the strongest part of his bond with the common people.

Phillips goes on to say that in his July 4, 1861, message to a special session of Congress:

Lincoln reaffirmed his most deeply held beliefs, all of which had sprung from sentiments embodied in the Declaration of Independence:

"This is essentially a people's contest. On the side of the Union, it is a struggle for maintaining in the world that form and substance of government whose leading object is to elevate the condition of men—to lift artificial weights from all shoulders—to clear the paths of laudable pursuit for all—to afford all an unfettered start, and a fair chance, in the race of life."

Lincoln's leadership was the embodiment of who he was as a person; from his humble beginnings to his genuine passion and belief in hope, "for all time to come."

It was because of who he was, how *personally connected* he was to his authentic self, how he let this authenticity shine through his leadership, how much he cared for his fellow "common man," and the vision he was committed to bringing to life that Lincoln became so revered. As Phillips remarks:

Such inspirational words from the nation's chief executive could not help but move people, especially the common man who was the foot soldier during the Civil War. They revered Lincoln, trusted him, cheered him loudly wherever he went.

The typical Union soldier enjoyed a bond with the president that few people in American history have ever had with a sitting United States president. That bond began in Washington in early 1861, when Lincoln got out of the "ivory tower" of the White House and personally visited many of the arriving troops destined for the front.

Lincoln set the standard for leaders being the most adamant steward of values for their organizations when he "resurrected the Declaration of Independence, dusted off the Constitution, and brought back a sense of pride and patriotism that had not been seen since the days of the American Revolution. Lincoln revitalized the old values of Americanism and reminded all citizens why the United States was formed in the first place...

And finally, Lincoln laid out his ultimate vision for the country when he gave the speech that changed the course of history:

...that we here highly resolve that these dead shall not have died in vain; that this nation, under God, shall have a new birth of freedom; and that government of the people, by the people, for the people, shall not perish from the earth.

Lincoln was the leader the country needed to survive. It was his connection to his own self, to the true greatness of his country, and to his country's founding values and principles, fortified by his ability to lead from within himself that made Lincoln the leader destined to save our republic.

Abraham Lincoln is our country's eternal legacy of Character-Based Leadership.

Glen Senk, CEO of Urban Outfitters

One CEO I admire profusely for being so connected to, and honest about, his vision, values and personal character is Glen Senk of Urban Outfitters.

Living an Authentic Life

In an interview with Glen by Knowledge@Wharton that was published May 25, 2011, Glen was quoted as saying (after a reference to him successfully battling cancer in 1989), "You realize you have to take responsibility for doing what is right for you. You have to live a life you want to lead."

Senk added that focusing on living what he calls an "authentic" life has paid huge dividends. "A lot of my friends who went on to be very successful in investment banking or law or consulting... are not as happy as I am. There is not a day that I don't wake up bounding out of bed and can't wait to get to work."

The Power of Personal Vision

The words "You have to live a life you want to lead" are some of the most powerful that one can express, believe in, and commit to as a leader. Glen knew relatively early on that his vision meant following his passion for the retail industry, of which he said, "I love the theater of retail. I love that I can control every part of the experience—the product itself, the pricing, the way the product is sold, the way we communicate and so on."

The fact that he was so committed to this vision that he applied for a job at Bloomingdale's *46 times* before landing a job with them speaks volumes about the power, and compelling nature, of his personal vision. This vision also played a role later in his career when he took a risk and left Williams-Sonoma to work for Richard Hyne at Urban:

> I went from supervising 200 people, having two assistants and flying on the Concorde [at Williams-Sonoma] to running one store that did less than $1 million. **I had a vision for myself and what it could be.** And I believed so strongly in the culture [Hayne] had created at Urban.

Culture and Diversity

Knowledge@Wharton says Senk described the culture at Urban as one where creative, collaborative and curious people are given the freedom to operate almost like entrepreneurs:

> Diversity—including diversity of race, religion and political views—is also central to that vision. "Dick Hayne is a Republican," Senk noted. "I'm the first openly gay CEO of a Fortune 1,000 company....We believe as a company in hiring diversity, not because it is politically correct, but because diversity makes us stronger. I look for people who complement me, not [people] who look at the world the same way that I do."

I believe that an understanding of, and commitment to, a culture that demonstrates the values you profess is a critical result of Character-Based Leadership. Leaders demonstrate their true character by being the foremost steward of company values, and by imbuing the corporate culture with those values.

One should give honest consideration to whether it makes sense to work at a company where your values do not match the leader's.

As Glen points out with poignant truth, "If it is not a culture fit, you probably will not do well. Spend time in the lunch room, spend time with the receptionist—spend time with the real people in the organization if you want to know what the culture is really like."

Glen is an eloquent example of a CEO who is genuinely connected to who he is at his deepest and most personal level, and who is committed to his personal vision, purpose and values. He brings this connection and commitment to his role as CEO.

Glen sets a brilliant example of leading authentically from within, the pinnacle of Character-Based Leadership.

Martin Luther King Jr.

One only needs to read the following quote documented by Mervyn A. Warren and Gardner C. Taylor in the book *King Came Preaching: The Pulpit Power of Dr. Martin Luther King Jr.* to understand the depth of connection that Dr. Martin Luther King Jr. had to himself and the world around him:

> All I'm saying is simply this, that all life is interrelated, that somehow we're caught in an inescapable network of mutuality tied in a single garment of destiny. Whatever affects one directly affects all indirectly. For some strange reason, I can never be what I ought to be until you are what you ought to be. You can never be what you ought to be until I am what I ought to be. This is the interrelated structure of reality.

Dr. King's ability to preach a belief so enlightened and rooted in the interconnectedness we all share demonstrates an understanding of the imperative for us all to succeed, for us all to transform unto our higher selves, for the good of all. Leading by transforming from within and encouraging others to transform from within is genuinely at the core of Character-Based Leadership.

This desire to see the people of the world transform from within was at the crux of Dr. King's mission, for which he toiled unrelentingly and for which he won a Nobel Peace Prize for promoting nonviolent social change. Although his objective was to garner civil rights change and legislation in America, and his mission was to promote social change in a nonviolent way, his vision is eloquently laid out in his "I Have a Dream" speech:

> ...one day right there in Alabama, little black boys and black girls will be able to join hands with little white boys and white girls as sisters and brothers.... One day even the state of Mississippi, a state sweltering with the heat of injustice, sweltering with the heat of oppression, will be transformed into an oasis of freedom and justice... [and]... my four little children will one day live in a nation where they will not be judged by the color of their skin but by the content of their character.

This gives color, starkness, truth and emotion to King's ultimate vision. Ultimately, these words all represent a world where the people, as a whole, have transformed at their highest level. This is leadership at an enlightened level.

In summary, the cornerstone of Character-Based Leadership, as demonstrated here by three of our country's most brilliant leaders, is formed by a divine connection to our inner selves at our deepest and most personal levels; an understanding of whence we came, keeping us grounded; an inspired personal vision; a set of strong and respectful values; and an enlightened vision of where we want to lead others.

From this starting point, we can truly change the world!

Chapter 6

Leading from Our Strengths

Page Cole

I walked up on a conversation between my dad and the janitor one evening as my dad was asking him about each of his kids and calling them by name. That may not seem like a big deal, but it is. The janitor happened to work at the university where my dad had served as president for 17 years. Dad had recently retired and was back for the dedication of a $24 million Fine Arts building. Raising funds and building this facility had been the focus of his final years as president. We were leaving early because my dad was feeling poorly, having recently been diagnosed with cancer. But on what was a huge night for him, at a time when he was feeling poorly, he stopped for a moment to check on a former employee. I wasn't really that surprised. I'd seen my dad invest in people his entire life. This was just who he was. He died six months later. The governor in our state ordered flags flown at half-mast on the day of his funeral. For over 30 years, my dad had rubbed shoulders with world leaders like Mikhail Gorbachev and President Bush Sr., and invested through education in students like Blake Shelton, the country music star. My dad personally knew governors and politicians from around the country and had grown his university through millions of dollars of buildings and program development. But these were not his greatest achievements.

Months after his death, my mother went to Wal-Mart and was stopped at the door by the greeter. "I just miss Dr. Cole so much," the greeter said. With tears running down her cheek, she shared, "He always stopped to talk to me, and I just miss the hugs he gave." The story repeated itself over and over, from bank tellers, neighbors, colleagues and church pastors. Comments varied from "He was such a positive person" to "He believed in me more than anyone else in my life ever has." The theme was always the same. My dad led from his strength… the strength of investing in and believing in others. My dad modeled what it meant to be a Character-Based Leader and to lead from his greatest strength.

Knowing that not everyone in leadership is a Character-Based Leader, one question in particular needs to be answered. Are we Character-Based Leaders because we lead from our strengths, or do we lead from our strengths because we are Character-Based Leaders? To find this out, we have to understand what it means to lead from our strengths, recognizing and avoiding those ineffective alternatives to leading from our strengths, and why it's critically important for us as Character-Based Leaders to lead from our strengths.

What Does It Mean to Lead from Your Strengths?

Accepting Your Value as a Leader

Ask any person in leadership what it means to "lead from your strengths," and you may get more different answers to the question than the number of people you ask the question. I believe that leading from your strengths can't be narrowed down to one definition or explanation, but that it has many facets. First on this list is that you're honest and brave enough to affirm that you, just like everyone else, are good at something! It's amazing how many people believe that leadership is reserved for only a very few, and that those few are the exceptionally gifted ones on the planet. This thinking couldn't be further from the truth! Leading from your strengths requires you to accept the truth that you're a good leader! You're further down the road of life, more experienced, gifted or insightful than others you will encounter, and they need your leadership to help them develop and grow.

Discovering Your Unique Leadership Strengths

Leading from your strengths is more than just admitting you are good at something. It also involves the next phase of leadership, discovering what it is that you do really well. The challenge for leaders is that this is less like a mining expedition and more like working in a laboratory. John Quincy Adams said, "If your actions inspire others to dream more, learn more, do more and become more, you are a leader." Everyone has the ability to help someone else dream, learn, do or become more than they are. So in reality, everyone is a leader!

It is time-consuming and worthless to dig around haphazardly in your life to discover where your strengths lie. Instead, it's your job to "get into the lab" and determine for yourself what you do best as a leader. You do this in several ways. First, look at your leadership experiences by asking, "What am I best at helping people do that enables them to become better than they are today?" Is it helping them develop a vision, learn or sharpen their skills, or work the task, or is it encouraging them to grow personally? Or is it something altogether different? Next, ask the people you've led and the people who have led you what they think your strengths are as well. Finally, if you're still unsure about those strengths, then experiment! It's the way most great discoveries are made, and the potential for what you will find is life-altering!

Moving from Mediocre to Magnificent

Living an average life may be okay with some people, but it shouldn't be okay with Character-Based Leaders. Accepting an assessment of yourself as being "average" among leaders is nothing more than a confession that you are comfortable with being a poorer leader than 50% of the leaders in your arena. Character-Based Leaders know differently and are convinced that they can be more, be better, and be excellent at what they are doing. Age and experience are irrelevant to this discussion. It doesn't

> *Living an average life may be okay with some people, but it shouldn't be okay with Character-Based Leaders.*

matter if you're fresh out of college or in the golden years of your life. Moving your strengths from good to excellent and cutting away the nonessentials to make room for developing strengths into expertise is a hallmark of the Character-Based Leader.

Contagious Inspiration

Lao Tzu said it best. "Go to the people. Learn from them. Live with them. Love them. Start with what they know. Build with what they have. But with the best leaders when the job is done, the task accomplished, the people will say 'We have done this ourselves.'" Leading from your strengths doesn't mean bossing others or demanding your way because you're better, bigger or more influential than they are. Instead, the Character-Based Leader is committed to inspiring others to discover their own strengths. This entails equipping others to transform their good to excellence, their strengths into expertise, and then in turn teaching them how to pay it forward by doing the same for other growing leaders.

What Are the Alternatives to Leading from Our Strengths?

Not all organizations or leaders are committed to leading from their strengths. They dislike the idea of giving leaders the ability to lead from their strengths. Instead, they prefer alternative forms of leadership and consider anything else to be foolish, ineffective or terrifying. But if we're going to lead from our strengths as Character-Based Leaders, we need to recognize and understand the counterfeit styles of leadership that stand in stark contrast to strengths-based leadership.

Leading by Position

"I'll do what I can do whether it's my strength or not because I'm the boss. I have earned the right to choose, and it's irrelevant if my quality of performance is poor or if someone else's performance in that area is exceptional compared to mine. Position, not strengths, will determine who leads."

We often think of the CEO of a large corporation when this style is mentioned, but it can just as easily be found in the small business run locally by a prominent family in the business community. The most obvious challenge of this style is that because skill or expertise is not a necessary requirement to be in charge, the organization may not have the most effective or strongest leader at the helm.

Leading by Policy

"I'll do what I have to do under my job title, because those are the rules. The structure and guidelines are more important than the people and results. I'm not sticking my neck out at any time, for anyone or any reason. Let the policies lead us."

Large groups or institutions can become overwhelmed with concern about lawsuits, perceived lack of fairness or impartiality, or just plain laziness. In an attempt to deal with growth, change or conflict, policies are instituted to apply across the board to people and situations that arise. But situations, people, organizations and life itself all continually change, making many policies quickly outdated or unfair. The result is an automated structure without vision, flexibility or passion. In this setting, it doesn't matter what your strengths are, only if you're following policy.

Leading by Preference

"I'll do what I want to do, because I want to enjoy myself. Results are secondary to my own personal pleasure."

Although leading from our strengths usually does have some measure of enjoyment or fulfillment attached to it, leading by preference puts everything else as secondary to the selfish goal of achieved narcissism. What strengths-based leadership does *not* do is allow us to lead for our own pleasure at the expense of others or at the cost of failure for the cause or organization. Leading from our strengths doesn't inconsiderately trample on the efforts or goals of others like leading by preference consistently does.

Leading by Participation

"I'll do what everyone else in the group thinks I should do so that there is a perceived environment of equality and fairness."

There is an inherent danger in talking about leading from our strengths. The danger manifests itself when individuals begin to incorrectly assess the areas of inadequacy or weakness in each other as strengths, and then unqualified leaders assume leadership in areas where they are not strong. This is especially prevalent in organizations where positions of leadership are determined by elections or by popularity. Strengths-based leadership, in contrast, is able to separate friendship from fact and to distinguish likeability from leadership ability. Those organizations that successfully navigate those options enlist and assign leadership to those most qualified to lead without any deference based on friendship or relationship.

Leading by Pandemonium

"I'll lead where I want, and the rest can fight, grab or subvert the areas where they want to lead. Whoever wins out in the battle for leadership in an area is the one who deserves to lead, whether they are the best performer or not."

We see this kind of dog-eat-dog attitude prominently in action in many workplaces. This is the attitude that would vehemently defend the adage that the ends justify the means. Success for the individual in this setting is much more important than success for the organization or for other individuals.

Pandemonium-based leadership also includes leading by abdication. This type of leadership detaches itself from the organization, not genuinely caring what anyone else does. Its leader would take a laissez faire attitude, maintaining that he or she is not responsible for anyone, not even their own leadership or actions. Strengths-based leadership contends just the opposite, advocating that we are each responsible for leading from our own areas of strength, and for helping others to discover and lead from their strengths as well.

Leading by Personality

"I'll do what I can to charm and convince everyone, whether I can deliver the results needed or not."

Finally, this counterfeit style of leadership is driven purely by personality. Success, skill, education and expertise are ignored in favor of the charisma of the leader. This leader is relational in nature and, in truth, that may be their greatest strength, but this relational strength can be abused to convince others to allow the unqualified or ineffective leader to guide or shape the organization and its efforts in areas where this leader shouldn't. Strengths-based leadership instead places people in areas of leadership without consideration to whether or not they have winsome personalities. Leadership is driven by results and not by smooth talking or physical attractiveness.

Why Is It Important That We Lead from Our Strengths?

Biggest Bang for the Leadership Buck

Leading from your greatest strengths is where you'll find your greatest results. Let's be honest. Performance is crucial, and it's usually the primary measuring stick when it comes to leadership that makes a difference. With limits on time, manpower, finances and every other resource you might imagine, the organization wants and needs the greatest return on investment (ROI) from leadership that it can get. Organizations are more successful when they have people who lead from their strengths.

These same principles of leading from your strengths hold true for you as an individual. If you spend more time working on your weaknesses than on leading from your strengths, you will be less effective as a leader. Do what only you can do, and do it exceptionally well.

The Right Tool for the Right Job

Leading from our strengths is who we're designed to be. Many in Character-Based Leadership believe that each of us is designed with a unique divine thumbprint that has rolled across our lives, giving us greater purpose in finding and then using our strengths to lead.

Proverbs 22:6 says, "Train up a child in the way he should go, and when he is old, he will not depart from it." This teaching has long been explained as meaning that if we teach our kids to be nice, they'll grow up nice. If we teach them kindness, fair play and hard work, when they move out into the real world, they'll be good citizens that we're proud of. The problem with that interpretation is simple... **It's wrong**. This verse actually translates, "Train up a child in the way he is 'bent,' and when he is old, he will not depart from it." In a nutshell, we're told to discover the bent, the inclination, the strength of our kids, and then to foster and encourage those strengths, because it's those things that truly make up who our kids divinely intended to be! Only when families, schools, mentors and leaders begin to invest in young leaders using this principle will we see a huge long-term effect in the quality and quantity of strengths-based leadership.

Your Kids Look Just Like You

Leading from your strengths naturally produces more effective mentoring relationships. It's a simple organic principle. Orange trees produce oranges, Bengal tigers produce Bengal tiger cubs, and, as exciting or as frightening as it may be, leaders typically produce leaders who look just like them as leaders. If you are weak in confronting problems with staff, but insist on holding on to this responsibility, those leaders you mentor will also make those same poor decisions regarding conflict resolution with staff.

People thrive when following a performing leader, someone they can believe in. These are the kinds of leaders produced from mentoring relationships led by strengths-based leaders, where young leaders have an effective model of leading from their strengths to model their own leadership after. This is in stark contrast to those who are forced to follow a positional leader with authority by virtue of title and no substantial success or quality of performance.

Whether they want to or not, many people will mirror key characteristics of those leaders they follow. If you're a leader who leads from your strengths and enjoys the success that follows, the people you lead will most likely follow suit and become the same kind of leaders. If you don't lead primarily from your strengths, then your "leadership progeny" will follow suit and fail miserably.

Timing Is Critical in Leadership

Finally, it's important to Character-Based Leadership that we lead from our strengths, because leading from our strengths puts us ahead of the problems and the competition we face. Strengths-based leaders stay out in front of the learning curve that other leaders encounter when forced to lead in an area of weakness. Leading from our strengths also allows us to use the bulk of our time genuinely leading instead of groping our way blindly or with uncertainty through the challenges facing us as leaders.

Time is a fixed quantity. We can hire more staff and gather more tangible resources, but it's impossible to make any more time. Therefore, the responsibility is on you as the leader to get the greatest ROI from each moment and each experience that you invest in as a leader. It is understood that leaders are always learning. Good leaders never stop learning. But the less "on-the-job training" you're receiving as the leader and the more leading from your strengths you are doing, the more effective you'll be in attaining lasting results and quality relationships.

How Do We Become Leaders Who Lead from Our Strengths?

The case has been made regarding the importance of leading from our strengths. We've also seen the failures of counterfeit leadership styles to measure up against the success of strengths-based leadership, and why it's critically important for Character-Based Leadership that we lead from our strengths. So now the question remains, "How do we become leaders who lead from our strengths?"

Since every situation is unique, made up of a multitude of factors, personalities and circumstances, there is no simple and easy procedure for making this happen. I'm not sure anyone could direct people to follow just one pattern for strengths-based leadership exactly and promise them success. Rather than giving an exclusive and inflexible set of "commandments" for you to follow, consider these "10 Considerations" for leading from our strengths.

I. **Reflection: "Consider thou a view of thy track record."**
    Do an honest self-evaluation of your past leadership opportunities. Look for those areas where you have succeeded

not only in your performance, but also in leading others to grow and perform.

II. **Inspection: "Consider asking thy people what they thinketh."**
Ask for critiques of your performance as a leader from people who would know (mentors, other leaders, and your followers) and whom you trust to be brutally honest with you.

III. **Retrospection: "Consider thy faults and how thou mightst avoid them."**
You've looked for your strengths, but you should also look for your weaknesses. Learning which areas to stay out of and to give away is just as important as learning where to step up and lead.

IV. **Dissection: "Consider thy load, and give each his portion to carry."**
Maybe there are some parts that you are good at and that need your expertise, but not everything. Break the process or project into smaller parts, and keep only those parts that need your attention.

V. **Selection: "Consider the delegation of thy weakness unto another with strength."**
There is simply too much to do in most of our situations for one person to do it all. You must get both comfortable and adept at delegating the right task to the right person for overall success to be achieved. Keep what you're good at and give the rest of it away to others with strengths in those areas.

VI. **Resurrection: "Consider restoration of thy dreams and joys."**
You may have stopped doing something you were great at doing. Circumstances, job change, health and financial considerations are just a few of the reasons people quit leading from their strengths. Find a way to bring these opportunities back to life so you can lead from your strengths.

VII. **Deflection: "Consider that all should be treated fairly, but not equally, since not all are equal."**
Not every emergency or perceived crisis deserves your time and attention. Not all jobs are equal in their importance, preference or place on the timeline. Put off those that don't fall within your strength set if they are not time-critical. There may not be someone else right now who can deal with those issues, but there

very well may be some time or additional resources down the road.

VIII. **Rejection: "Consider cutting off the stuff that offends thee."**
There are some things that you as the leader need to be brave and insightful enough to cut out completely. Not every idea is a good idea, and not every task conceived is one that is worth being completed. As the leader, don't be afraid to hit the delete button!

IX. **Affection: "Consider that thou canst do what thou lovest and lovest what thou dost."**
If you're not doing what you love, it probably means you're not leading from your strengths. It's finding that sweet spot where your passion and your performance connect that will bring you the greatest success and satisfaction in life.

X. **Perfection: "Consider that time is thy servant, not thy master."**
OK, perfection isn't going to happen, but you can be closer to it than you are right now! Prioritize your time when it comes to your roles and activities. A modest starting goal for a leader would be to determine that at least 51% of your time be spent leading from your strengths. An admirable goal to work toward would be that 80% of your time is spent leading from those strengths...

Leading from our strengths is a dynamic and necessary facet to Character-Based Leadership. So what is the answer to the question posed earlier? Are we Character-Based Leaders because we lead from our strengths, or do we lead from our strengths because we are Character-Based Leaders? The answer is simple. Yes, we are.

> *The greater a man is in power above others, the more he*
> *ought to excel them in virtue. None ought to govern who*
> *is not better than the governed.*
> **~ Publius Syrus**

Chapter 7

Using Your Head to Manage and Your Heart to Lead

Jane Perdue

The main ingredient of good leadership is good character. This is because leadership involves conduct and conduct is determined by values.
~ **General Norman Schwarzkopf**

Spencer, the new CFO, was intense. Water cooler wisdom had it that after three weeks on the job, he hadn't yet smiled at anyone. His fondness for demanding project requests with short deadlines was already legend. Yet it wasn't until he threw a six-inch-thick binder completely across a four-foot-wide table that we knew his number one priority was getting the job done, period.

It's still debated today whether his book toss, as it's been labeled, was an ugly expression of unchecked anger or a deliberate act aimed at the VP who had tactfully declined to do the work Spencer had just assigned. After I tried to offer some peer-to-peer feedback to him during a break in that tense, unfriendly meeting and experienced his response, I surmised that his behavior was most deliberate. Spencer did not regret his action and was, in fact, surprised that people had been offended. He expressed extreme disgust with my proffered coaching as well as utter disdain for the VP who doubted his financial sagacity. Spencer declared me a fool for thinking that an apology was in order. He viewed his response simply as doing his job, and the rest of us as obviously not doing ours. That's when I realized Spencer had no moral center. The plus side of his character account carried a zero balance.

The good news is that Spencer's stay in the company was brief, only eight eternity-like months. His grow-the-bottom-line-at-any-cost orientation was polarizing. Some people saw him as the savior, the one who would catapult the company to first-place dominance in the industry; others viewed him as a cancer, concerned that his take-no-prisoners style would spread far, wide and deep across the organization, resulting in employees being seen as a robotic means to achieve a profit-oriented end.

In retrospect, both camps had it wrong. Everyone either forgot or didn't realize that a Character-Based Leader uses his head to manage *and* his heart to lead. The pro-Spencer corner was all task-focused. The anti-Spencer crew was stuck in fostering friendships. This either/or approach misses the mark. Character-Based Leadership sees the importance of both results and relationships.

Task completion and relationship building have been thoroughly researched. The Ohio State University sponsored studies on structure versus consideration, and the University of Michigan sponsored leadership behavior studies on employee versus production-orientation. Hersey and Blanchard published the situational model of leadership. Blake and Mouton offered the managerial grid. James MacGregor Burns introduced transactional and transformational leadership. Robert K. Greenleaf coined servant leadership. B. F. Skinner, Jean Piaget, and Konrad Lorenz duked out the nature-versus-nurture arguments. Fiedler advanced the contingency aspects of leadership. Peter Drucker coined the phrase "knowledge worker," raising awareness of people who work with information. There are leadership traits, theories and lists galore. It's all great stuff, yet it's all worthless if someone is like Spencer and lacks a moral center.

> *"I used to think that running an organization was equivalent to conducting a symphony orchestra. But I don't think that's quite it; it's more like jazz. There is more improvisation."*
> ~ *Warren Bennis*

There must be a sense of "being" good in all the "doing" well. Sean T. Hannah and Bruce Avolio sum it up when they describe leadership as a "sense of ownership over the ethical conduct of oneself." That's the heart of Character-Based Leadership: a knowledge and love of the good through which one creates positive and sustainable change, using one's head to manage and one's heart to lead, regardless of job title or level within an organization.

> *We need leaders who lead with purpose, value, and integrity; leaders who build enduring organizations, motivate their employees to provide superior customer service, and create long-term value for shareholders.*
> ~ ***Bill George***, *former head of Medtronic and author*

Given that you are reading this book, I suspect you may have discovered that being a Character-Based Leader can be a worthwhile yet sometimes lonely state. The business world is rife with organizations in which immoral, unethical and even illegal behavior is openly accepted or allowed in a wink-wink, leave-room-for-plausible-deniability atmosphere. Perhaps you work at an organization where the sole focus is profit, a focus that leaves you feeling empty. Perhaps you are at a juncture in your life where you value people, principles and profits, and are searching for a way to breathe life, meaning and tangible results into all three. You know that getting the job done and connecting with people are essential leadership dimensions, and you want to do them with honor, integrity, and goodness.

So where does one start the journey to becoming a Character-Based Leader, becoming someone who values both task completion and relationship building within the workplace and who strives to achieve both? I'm fond of saying that to lead others, to think more of *we* and less of *me*, one must start with oneself. I suggest beginning your Character-Based Leadership journey by getting grounded in three concepts:

- valuing both tasks and relationships,
- being an inclusive thinker, and
- exercising positive character in leadership.

Valuing Both Tasks and Relationships

> *Leadership is a matter of intelligence, trustworthiness, humaneness, courage and discipline. Reliance on intelligence alone results in rebelliousness. Exercise of*

humaneness alone results in weakness. Fixation on trust results in folly. Dependence on the strength of courage results in violence. Excessive discipline and sternness in command result in cruelty. When one has all five virtues together, each appropriate to its function, then one can be a leader. ~ **Sun Tzu**

Character-Based Leaders use their heads to manage and their hearts to lead. They deliver on both tasks *and* relationships. A head-and-heart-connected leader gets the work done and done well, inspiring employees, making them feel valued and connected to their organization. Both head and heart practices are absolutely vital to long-term business success, on both Wall Street *and* Main Street.

Much of value has been researched and written on defining management and leadership, so no definitions are provided here. Rather than haggling over what a leadership duty is versus a management one, I propose simply concentrating on people, principles and results, not getting hung up on labels. Thomas Watson Sr., who took IBM to its early levels of greatness, beautifully defines the business balance between head and heart: "To be successful, you have to have your heart in your business, and your business in your heart."

Although I'm eschewing definitions, I offer examples to help illustrate and clarify concepts. Task-focused work includes process and procedure, work flow and scheduling, record keeping and reporting, project management and compliance. The list goes on and on and represents the nitty-gritty planning, organizing, controlling and directing requirements of running a business.

Relationship-building practices touch people emotionally, even spiritually, and encompass workplace essentials like respect, recognition, two-way communication, collaboration and partnership, having fun, and feeling engaged. These practices create alignment between the business's mission and the employee's on-the-job behaviors.

There must be room in business for both task-oriented activities (making money, operational efficiency, etc.) and relationship-focused activities (compassion, trust, etc.). Employees bring their brains and their feelings with them to work each day, so it's only natural that the workplace should contain elements that use both brains and feelings.

During the Renaissance, art and science were both highly valued. However, with the advent of scientific management in the United States in the early twentieth century, work focus shifted to time-and-motion studies, standardization and concentration on tasks. Frederick Taylor, one of the intellectual leaders of the Efficiency Movement, sums up this scientific management orientation:

> It is only through enforced standardization of methods, enforced adoption of the best implements and working conditions, and enforced cooperation that this faster work can be assured. And the duty of enforcing the adoption of standards and enforcing this cooperation rests with management alone.

While few companies today are as completely rigid in coerced consistency as Taylor proposes, many are highly focused on earnings, at whatever the cost, as the recent recession so powerfully illustrates. Strong elements of task concentration still exist in today's workplaces as employees are considered expenses rather than assets on a company's balance sheet. David Whyte paints a bleak picture in *The Heart Aroused: Poetry and the Preservation of the Soul in Corporate America* when he writes:

> ...finding the soul in American corporate life is blessedly fraught with difficulties... any man or woman working in the pressure of a modern corporation is making their way through the world, but it may be a world that seems, as the years roll by, to have less and less room for soul.

A character-based, head-and-heart connected leader uses positive and powerful energy as well as impact and influence to assure this loss of soul does not happen. An authentic head-and-heart leader thinks "we" first, "me" second. He understands the business, has solid management acumen, and brings fun and laughter, adventure, unbounded possibility and inventive thinking to leading people and attaining shared visions.

If this person is a formal leader, someone holding a job title that involves overseeing the work of others, her department will be the one humming with productivity and high employee engagement. If the individual is an informal leader, someone who does not manage a department, function, or people, he will be the person whose involvement and counsel is sought out because people want to know what he thinks and feels about an issue. Head-and-heart connected leaders inspire everyone to be the best they can be.

Broad and Inclusive Thinking

Avoid the tyranny of the OR and embrace the genius of the AND.
~ James C. Collins and Jerry I. Porras, Built to Last

Society, academia and business have conditioned us to use primarily an either/or approach to thinking and reward us for doing so. Either/or problem-solving skills belong in every leader's toolkit, yet either/or thinking is only one component of the broad and inclusive mindset necessary for both achieving goal accomplishment and creating an atmosphere of trust and goodwill.

Either/or thinking is used when solving a problem that has a defined end point and an absolute answer: *Is Rebecca ready to be promoted? Do I major in psychology or business? What questions should be asked in our customer satisfaction survey?* Answering each of these questions may require assessing and evaluating multiple scenarios and variables, yet only one reaches a definitive answer, i.e., *Yes, Rebecca is ready to be promoted; or no, Rebecca isn't ready to be promoted because her conflict-resolution skills need more work.*

Consider Spencer and his six-inch-thick binder full of numbers, charts, and graphs. His default position was on task achievement. He operated in a one-way, one-dimensional outlook in which all systems, processes and procedures were singularly focused on task accomplishment: there's a job to be done, so just do it. He was incapable of understanding people who did not share his task orientation.

When leaders concentrate too much on either task or people, things start to go wrong. Typically, it's the task-oriented practices that get priority attention. Metrics like cash flow, widgets per hour, budgeted versus actual expenses, and the like are irrefutably logical. Although some may passionately argue about the numbers, numbers are dispassionate. There's no heart or soul in a marketing campaign analysis report in and of itself. Yet the author of the report has most likely contributed heartfelt emotion (particularly if he operates from a character-based foundation), e.g., *Did we talk to all the right people in pulling this report together? Have we captured all the angles? Will both the CEO and shop floor supervisor understand what we're saying? Will being honest with our findings help or end our careers?*

Having an appropriate balance of attention on task and relationship is best for both the business and employees, and is where the inclusive both/and thinking comes into play. Achieving task completion and relationship building requires a both/and orientation, commonly called a "polarity" because both outcomes are correct. Neither can successfully stand alone for the long term. Both are needed over time to optimize the situation. Leaders focus first on one, then the other, oscillating between the two as the circumstances require.

Positive Character in Head-and-Heart Leadership

[Transforming leadership] occurs when one or more persons engage with others in such a way that leaders and followers raise one another to higher levels of motivation and morality. ~ **James MacGregor Burns**

We suggest that the gap between knowing and doing what is right is partially explained by the concept of moral potency...which has three elements: moral ownership, moral courage and moral efficacy.
~ **Sean T. Hannah and Bruce J. Avolio,**
Moral Potency: Building the capacity for character-based leadership

Balancing the conflicts between selfish and selfless behavior is what a Character-Based Leader does every day. There's alignment between attitude, belief, and commitment. Attitude is one's pattern of emotions and actions, demonstrating an individual's tendency to favor a particular entity, person, thought, or feeling. Beliefs form the mental framework that one uses to form opinions, judgments and acceptance. Individuals then commit to making choices to think, act and behave in a certain and consistent way that's aligned with one's attitudes and beliefs.

Let's explore five tenets of knowing, being and doing that will serve you well on your Character-Based Leadership journey.

1. Be self-aware.

Becoming a character-based, head-and-heart-connected leader requires you first to make a personal commitment to understand, and then be able to manage, your own thoughts and feelings. The April 2003 *Harvard Business Review* article "Breakthrough Ideas for Tomorrow's Business Agenda" noted that the "reluctance to explore your inner landscape not only weakens your own motivation but can corrode your ability to inspire others." Before we can connect with others, we must first identify and then manage our own strengths and weaknesses. Once there's that level of personal mastery, leadership can spread throughout one's team, department, and organization.

Psychologist Daniel Goleman's work with emotional intelligence is highly instructive for individuals seeking self-understanding. As Goleman writes in *Vital Lies, Simple Truths*, "The range of what we think and do is limited by what we fail to notice. And because we fail to notice that we fail to notice, there is little we can do to change until we notice how failing to notice shapes our thoughts and deeds." Getting in touch with what we fail to notice about ourselves and others is a crucial first step in becoming a head-and-heart-connected leader.

Ask people for feedback. Look for patterns in the advice you have received over the years and then act on what you discover. Spencer had repeatedly been counseled to improve his people skills, yet he never opted voluntarily to do so, a fact I learned only after he had left the organization.

2. Embrace ethical norms and behavioral ideals.

A colleague of mine, Elizabeth, tells an enlightening story of being asked to artificially depict call center statistics during a presentation to corporate executives who would be visiting her area. Elizabeth's boss instructed her to describe performance as being within company standards when, in truth, the results fell far short of specified targets. It was Elizabeth's first month with the organization. She had left a prestigious job with a national firm to take this new position, attracted to handling the turnaround situation.

Aghast at being asked to tell a performance story that wasn't true and cognizant of her short tenure, Elizabeth stood her ground. She told her boss that lying served no one's interests and would, in fact, critically hamper efforts at improvements (not to say what dire implications existed for being found out). Why would the corporation fund millions of dollars in technology, training and facilities if all was well?

She convinced her boss that telling the truth was the right thing to do and was really a more compelling story; that she had left a prominent job in a well-known organization to take on the challenge of improving customer service and wanted to engage all levels of the company in devising and implementing the solution. Elizabeth's moral center prevailed. (So did her work in turning around customer service.)

3. Engage the world and perform beyond self-interest.

There's a special allure in being known as the one who solved a challenging problem or created something new. Yet these individual spotlight opportunities are rare; usually, it requires many such opportunities to create change. The truth is that the best answers usually result when one throws the doors of participation wide open, inviting everyone to engage.

Spencer could have learned a thing or two about performing beyond self-interest from Mike Henry Sr., president of the Lead Change Group, the chief instigator of a body of work resulting in this book. Mike had a vision that the world needed more Character-Based Leaders. He could have forged ahead alone, writing books, giving speeches, and spreading the word. Instead, he engaged the world, encouraging others who shared a similar view to join a movement. Mike embraced the power of open-source collaboration and of many voices involved in spreading a positive message of transformation. Transcending ourselves is at the heart of character.

4. Treat people as ends, not as means.

Years ago, I had a boss, Steve, who was more task-oriented than Spencer was. Steve viewed people not as individuals, but as elements of an emotionless system designed and expected to produce outcomes. His secretary said she believed he thought of her, if he thought of her at all, as being no different than the filing cabinet that stood in the corner, something utilitarian, a cog in the wheel of results.

I can't help but contrast Steve to George, another boss of mine. Everyone agreed that George was tough. He was demanding, settling for nothing less than everyone's best. He was goal-oriented, charismatic and driven. He pushed when outcomes weren't up to par; he beamed when they were. He challenged when he knew people were capable of more. He offered up praise, appreciation and thanks. He had his team's back. George understood tough empathy.

Fast-forward ten years. Do you want a he-made-me-feel-like-a-filing-cabinet legacy or something more meaningful, like "She caringly pushed me to levels I never knew I was capable of?"

5. *Envision both what is and what can be.*

A forward-thinking charter that engages one's mind and moves one's heart is a powerful combination, one that few individuals can resist. Leadership is a form of "power with" people, one that moves people beyond self-interest and locks them into a quest for the good of the group, organization, society, or some combination of the three.

Had Spencer understood the power of relationship building, perhaps his quest to make the company an industry leader might have succeeded. If he had created the intellectual and emotional stimulation where everyone could readily see the benefits that would accrue to employees, customers, shareholders and the company by charting a new path, people would have signed on in droves. Instead, he came across as a self-serving money-grubber, an unappealing position having no charm, pull or positive character.

> *"In the leadership arena, character counts."*
> *~ Warren Bennis*

Chapter 8

The Choices We Make

Tara R. Alemany

Every person living on this planet, from the newborn to the dying, has one very significant thing in common: Whether they are rich or poor, failures or successes, strong or weak, leaders or followers, they have choices to make every day.

Some people live their lives like human bumper cars, bouncing off those around them, sometimes changing their trajectory (and others'), while rarely making any conscious choices about what happens next.

Others see the endless stream of choices stretching out before them over the course of their lives and let panic set in,

> *Character-Based Leaders, like most leaders, recognize that life is full of choices, and they're willing to make them.*

paralyzing them. They ultimately "choose" to do nothing because fear of making the *wrong* choice keeps them from making any choice at all. So, they let life take its course, hoping for the best possible outcome, but doing little to affect it.

Then there are those who embrace life with all of its challenges and accomplishments. They wake up each day recognizing that decisions, both big and small, will need to be made and feeling equipped, or at least prepared, to make them. They recognize that some of the decisions they make will be the wrong ones. There's no way to avoid that. But they've learned how to keep the wrong decisions in perspective and that every decision made opens up a whole new set of choices.

Where does the Character-Based Leader fall along this spectrum of decision-makers? This individual is a special breed of decision-maker, perhaps one we could call the "ultra-decision-maker." The Character-Based Leader practices a unique skill that I call "intentionality."

Unlike the Human Bumper Cars or the Panicked Paralytics, Character-Based Leaders, like most leaders, recognize that life is full of choices, and they're willing to make them. However, their very essence requires them to make a daily, sometimes moment-by-moment, choice: the choice to lead (and make decisions) from a place of character. This means leading in ways that accentuate all that is good about human beings: leading with honesty, integrity and a thought to the future effects, building relationships and valuing others, recognizing that the goals and dreams they aspire to can *never* be fulfilled without the help and support of those around them.

The Character-Based Leader must be intentional in making every decision. This means recognizing and taking into consideration all of the various effects that could possibly result from their decisions and going with the solution that has the most positive outcome for the largest number of people. This is why many Character-Based Leaders embrace the concept of servant leadership. They are often willing to sacrifice their own desired outcomes for the result that is best for everyone. They even allow others to make decisions about the direction the team is going in, recognizing that "the needs of the many outweigh the needs of the few, or the one" as Spock reminded us in the Star Trek movie *The Wrath of Khan*. As the leaders, however, they recognize when it is their duty to guide and direct, and when they need to allow others the freedom and responsibility to grow into leaders themselves.

Every moment of our lives is filled with choices. When I wake up in the morning, do I choose to be excited about the potential in this new day or overwhelmed by all that needs to get done? Do I recognize the difference between needs and wants so that I can prioritize my activities and decisions based on those that are more significant? When I go through the day, do I treat others with respect and listen to what they have to say or do I heedlessly attempt to get them to conform to my views? At the close of the day, as I look back on all that has passed, will I see that I have lived a day that I can look back on ten years from now without regrets? Did I spend time with my loved ones? Did I make the best possible decisions I could for myself and for the people around me? Did I accomplish something or make a difference in someone else's life?

Remember, at the end of it all, as we look back on our lives, no one is going to wish that they had mowed one more lawn, went shopping at one more store, watched one more TV show, made one more wall post on Facebook, or brokered one more deal before they died.

There is a song that I love by a Christian artist, Nicole Nordeman, called "Legacy." These lines in the song have always stood out for me:

> I won't lie, it feels alright to see your name in lights
> We all need an "Atta boy" or "Atta girl"
> But in the end I'd like to hang my hat on more besides
> The temporary trappings of this world
>
> I want to leave a legacy
> How will they remember me?
> Did I choose to love? Did I point to You enough
> To make a mark on things?

As Character-Based Leaders, we all have a legacy to make while we walk this earth. How will people remember you? Will they remember the extra time you spent with them to mentor them and lead them? Will they remember the respect, humility and integrity you invariably displayed? Will they look back and say, "Here was someone I always knew I could trust?" Will they count you not only as a leader, but also as a friend?

Be intentional about your choices. Start with the end in mind. What kind of legacy do you want to leave? What does it take to get there? What choices can you make right now, today, in this moment, that will start you in that direction?

Plan to succeed today. That's how it all begins…

Part III

Character-Based Leadership Traits

This section explores the various traits that are commonly considered necessary for Character-Based Leaders to exhibit. As we explore these traits and how they play out in our lives, it is our hope that you are inspired to find ways to apply them to your own life and leadership.

Integrity

Respect and Humility

Trust

Communication

Chapter 9

Walking the Walk

Heather Coleman-Voss

I am privileged. Not everyone gets the opportunity to walk the walk.
~ Lee Child, "Janet Salter" in 61 Hours

Recently, I had an experience that may have been classified as a nonevent by some and as a lucky moment by others. For me, it was a pivotal moment and one that has replayed itself often in my mind.

I was not charged for merchandise that I had purchased.

My husband and I were in a hurry to get to an important event of his. It was a long drive, and the event had a strict starting time. The heat was unbearable, we had miles to drive, our vehicle was loaded down with equipment, and we were, to put it lightly, stressed out. We had to make a stop at our local gas station; the line was long, the customer service clerk was young and new, and everyone was impatient. When I finally reached the counter, the young man smiled at me nervously and rang up the several items I laid on the counter.

"That'll be $18.60," he stated. I had a moment's confusion, anticipating the amount to be at least ten dollars more. He had started bagging up my items, and the line was continuing to grow behind me, so I shrugged, paid, and told him to have a nice day.

Making my way out of the store, I was doing the math in my head. Was there a sale of which I was unaware? Getting in the car, I announced that I thought I had been undercharged. My husband, eager to get moving, said, "For what we're paying in gas prices, and with what we spend here every week, they can afford it."

Yes, I thought, *that's true. The gas company can most certainly afford it. We just paid $60.00 to fill up the tank! If the clerk made a mistake, then that's more than covered by their huge profit margin. Okay, it's really not that big of a deal. What are ten or fifteen dollars to this company compared to real people struggling every day to just pay their bills?*

And through my rapid-fire justifications, *I felt it in my stomach.* The wrongness of what I was thinking, of what I was almost ready to do. I opened the door, to the surprise of my husband, who was starting the car. "I just can't do it," I said, feeling a lump rise in my throat.

When I reentered the store, the line was still long, the clerk still nervous, the people impatient. The seconds ticked by, our event looming over me. Still, I waited, and when I approached the clerk, he was surprised to see me again so soon. "Was something wrong with your order?" he asked hesitantly.

"No, actually, you undercharged me," I replied, "and I wanted to make sure that I pay what I owe you."

He looked at me oddly, found the store's receipt, and stopped cold. I will never forget the look on his face, one of confusion followed immediately by enormous relief. "I did undercharge you," he stated, looking directly at me, "and I'm new. I would have been in so much trouble. They would have taken this out of my check! I can't believe you came back! Most people wouldn't."

The people in the line behind me murmured their agreement, and the guy next to me said, "That's cool, what you did."

All the way to our event, I thought about this young man. The total he had undercharged me was $14.00, not a fortune, but to a young employee making minimum wage, paying that amount back to his employer would have had a big effect. I thought about how nice he was, how though he had been noticeably nervous, he was pleasant and professional. He was the type of employee who will make his employer proud. For a few moments, all I could think about was how glad I was that I had done the right thing.

Yay, me.

The truth is, what I have thought about since my first few moments of self-congratulation is just how easy it very nearly was for me to act without integrity, and what the ripple effect could have been. This friendly customer service representative was a pleasure to do business with. Had I skipped out on what I rightfully owed, his mistake notwithstanding, he would have had to feel the dread of telling his brand new-employer and feel the punishment of it in his first check, and he could have become known as the guy to "keep an eye on" rather than as a great new addition to the staff.

I know why I felt that sinking, sickening feeling in my stomach: because I almost chose to do something seemingly small and perhaps justifiable to some, which would have had a negative effect on this person. I would have been taking action in a way that is not consistent with the person I want to be. I can't very well parent my children authentically, be a leader at work, and write and speak about Character-Based Leadership if I am not living it even, or especially, with the small things. Character-Based Leadership is about the small moments when we make our decisions because they build the larger foundation of our integrity.

I am ashamed at just how close I came to acting in opposition to what I teach.

During our trip to our destination, I told my husband what had happened and my feelings about the experience. He had what he calls a V8

> *Character-Based Leadership is about making the right decisions not only in our work, but in our daily lives.*

moment. He had only been focused on getting to his important event on time. He hadn't even been thinking about the ramifications for this young man or how he had allowed his own stress to affect his own integrity.

The simple truth is that we cannot choose to live with integrity only when it is convenient for us. We cannot pretend that the little things don't matter as long as we are *saying* the right things, because it is our actions that count. Our decisions, large and small, determine who we are and who we will become. Character-Based Leadership is about making the right decisions not only in our work, but also in our daily lives.

For Character-Based Leaders, integrity becomes a part of every action. Integrity requires us to reframe our thinking when our thoughts do not align with our sense of self. Self-awareness, personal growth, and checking in with ourselves regularly are extremely important if we are to live the values we teach and model. Integrity becomes a part of every moment. It is only from this foundation that we can truly lead with character.

In other words, you can't choose when to have integrity.

Chapter 10

Exploring Integrity and Leadership

Mónica Díaz

Just what is integrity? We keep coming back to it if we talk about Character-Based Leadership. After all, any talk of character is incomplete without attention to honesty and honor, and there is no sense of being a leader of character without concordance between personal beliefs and actions.

I would like to begin by considering these three definitions of integrity from the *Oxford American Dictionary* in the context of leadership.

integrity |in□tegritē|

noun

1. the quality of being honest and having strong moral principles; moral uprightness : he is known to be a man of integrity.

2. the state of being whole and undivided : upholding territorial integrity and national sovereignty.

3. the condition of being unified, unimpaired, or sound in construction : the structural integrity of the novel.

I am sure that for many of us, honesty and strong moral principles are the *sine qua non* (absolutely necessary characteristics) of Character-Based Leadership. Honesty sounds simple enough, though we could dedicate volumes to the ways it goes unattended in current leadership practice.

But what about moral principles? We shy away, and understandably so I believe, from moralizing in the context of leadership training or discussions because moral arguments can be closely related to religious issues, cultural values, and extremist views of right or wrong. Moralizing usually does not present an inviting or compelling path to join in. It separates and alienates more than it helps, mainly because moralizing is usually about the I-am-right-and-you-are-wrong point of view. Let us step away from moralizing to explore what is moral in the leadership arena.

Perhaps we can find greater agreement if we focus on what makes leadership effective, sustainable, enriching and inviting, what brings out the best in each person involved. Likewise, we can strive to avoid all that proves ineffective, destructive, unsustainable and, in short, that which brings out the worst in us all. I know "best" and "worst" can still be a matter of debate, yet the easiest way for a leader to access the wisdom to tell the difference is by looking within.

If you or those you love could be on the other end of a leader's decision and agree with it, if you could live with the consequences and effects of that particular choice for the longest time, and if you would like to inherit what you are creating, then you are probably treading a moral high road. If you cannot see yourself experiencing this, or if you are unsure, there is definitely more to explore.

Moral principles are not about general assumptions; they are about everyday actions and conversations. They are about being brave enough to explore, to make mistakes, to correct course, and to ask the difficult questions of yourself and others. Can the next generations thrive after what we are doing now? Will we create possibility or lack of it? It is in the questions leaders ask themselves that moral principles come to life.

It must also be the whole leader who is doing the leading. The mind, heart, hands, and voice of the leader, when aligned to an inner purpose, will create a powerful message to share with others. Nothing is as destructive to leadership as incongruence. So, although nobody is truly perfect, Character-Based Leaders do strive for concordance between what they say and what they do. They seek for their minds to explore what their hearts long for. They listen and observe well because they know they can learn from existing examples what they want to breed or to limit within themselves.

There is really nothing like feeling true to yourself. We have all experienced it and honored it, even in the face of difficulty, even when it does not seem to be working. True alignment to purpose and principles leaves you feeling satisfied, ready to face the world and explore who you are. This dance between me and you, self-esteem and other-esteem only deepens and informs the way a leader sees the world and is better able to maintain integrity.

The benefits of integrity are threefold, at least! Integrity makes a leader strong and his message clear and easy to follow. Practicing integrity also feels right and is self-correcting for leaders who are willing to stay aware of themselves and the effects of their leadership.

As is the case with other subjects of this book, integrity is for many easier said than done. We don't really mean to make it sound like you need to be a saint, rather, just a leader

> *Character-Based Leaders strive for concordance between what they say and what they do.*

interested in coming as close as humanly possible to the ideal of integrity.

So let's explore a few ways to develop integrity in everyday leadership.

1. Know where you stand.

There is simply no way of being true to yourself if you do not know who you are. Even if you strive to remain honest, it will be difficult to do so when you are unaware of yourself. Awareness is the first step to being truthful, because if you know what lies within, you can learn how to be true to that and to others. If you do not know what lies within, every effort you make will fall short, mainly because what you have to offer is so limited, it is hidden from you and hard to access. This is why you must make knowing who you are and where you stand a lifelong journey.

There are no shortcuts, really, just self-reflection in any way you can find it, every single day. You can find yourself in prayer or meditation, in journaling and writing down your convictions, in conversation with others, in formal self-exploration techniques or programs. The act of living will present you with countless possibilities to see what you do and how you do it. Learn from that. Stay open to the learning and to your own unfolding.

Being a Human Element® practitioner has certainly helped me! It has aided me in understanding my own defensiveness and in moving through it. I constantly read on the subject, have trusted people who will call my bluff when they see it, and strive to remain open to the signs that I am moving away from myself. I know others who have found alternative paths to being in touch with themselves. Make sure you have found yours or are still actively looking.

You need to make your moral compass your own before you will be any good at expressing it in the world. A good way to achieve this is to go deep enough into your religion, practice or philosophy of life so that you understand it fully, live and breathe it, and embody it in who you are and where you stand.

2. Always respect your principles.

The key to this precept is in the word always. I mean that. Anything you may say or do that is counter to your principles is just not worth it. No matter who's asking, nothing will repay you for straying away from your own principles. Sometimes you may think that the moral high ground is for people who are already on the top. It is not. It is for you and me and everyone else on this planet. It will strengthen your resolve to lead and will show you creative ways to achieve your goals.

I also mean it when I say respect. You may not know how your principles got there or why they're important, but it is only by respecting your principles that you will be able to check them out, try them on for size, and understand if you need to transform them and why. I know that when I have strayed from my principles, it has been out of sheer insecurity, as if I was not worthy of having principles in the first place. I am worthy, as are you. We all are.

Here's a corollary for you: Do not ask others to betray their principles, either! Listen enough so that you may understand. If you cannot find common ground, stay respectful of both your principles and those of the people around you. There is a place for everyone, and it is not always together. In each of our individual missions, there are times when we meet and times when we drift apart. Handle it. It's a sad way to reinforce your values to shoot down the values of others. If they are not right, they are more likely to come around if you share what you believe rather than criticize what they hold true.

3. Learn to find your way back.

You not only don't need to be perfect, you just *can't*. It is in our nature to err. It is the most human of things to move unwittingly toward that which we have been trying to avoid. Integrity means also being able and willing to correct course.

The last thing you need to be ashamed of is being imperfect. Shame leads to greater shame to be unable to admit you were wrong and to correct what you can. In fact, I believe it is the most pervasive mistake for leaders to think they are always right. Especially when leaders become strong, the people around them tend to either believe the leader must be right or just pretend they believe it. That really doesn't do a leader any good.

If everyone is telling you how wonderful you are, you need to frequent other circles. Find trustworthy people who can tell you when they find fault in you. It doesn't mean they are right, but they will give you food for thought and preserve your sanity. After all, the best way back from a mistaken path is accompanied by people who care and understand your true intentions. Find those people and treasure their honesty, making it safe for them to freely express any concerns and observations they may have of you.

4. Put yourself first.

Coming from the author of *Otheresteem*, putting yourself first might seem like an oxymoron, but I assure you, it is not. True leadership is service. It takes others into consideration and works to improve their lives or it will not be sustainable and moral in the way we have defined above. Still, you cannot serve others if you do not put yourself first, set a good example, and remain fit to lead.

Forgetting yourself will not assist you in knowing where you stand. There is no way a person who wishes to lead with integrity can separate his or her own welfare from that of others. I feel very strongly that true leadership is not about sacrifice, but about sharing a common vision and having the strength to see it through.

Of course, there is a place for sacrifice, and there may be a time when leaders would need to put themselves in harm's way to do the right thing. The choice to do that is ever present, and I, as many others, have admired people for their willingness to make hard choices. But those leaders were not purposefully looking for sacrifice. They chose it over a terrible alternative when they were convinced that there was no better way. They found themselves brave enough to make that choice and secure in the fact that another leader would take up where they left off. In the course of most of our lives, we will not be faced with that extreme a choice, nor should we as leaders seek it.

A leader's life is one of example. What do you want your followers to learn from you? To me, leading is the ultimate act of love, and when you love those who follow, you want the very best for them. A true leader will both want this and exemplify this for the people he leads, by having their best interests in mind and by showing how they can take effective care of themselves. Part of what has made past leadership unsustainable is this idea of sacrifice as central to leadership. Character-Based Leaders love to help others. They love to live in accordance with their own principles; it is pure joy to do so, and not a sacrifice in any way.

I cannot conceive of a direct path to integrity that would sacrifice self-integrity. Wholeness. Aliveness. Wellness. Isn't that what leaders are here for? I want to see my leaders take care of themselves well, to understand themselves. And then, we can truly believe they will care about us all, about the world. We can see them as living proof that we can live differently, live well, and love who we are and what we can help others to be.

Chapter 11

Mastering the Inner Game of Personal Integrity

Susan Mazza

When it comes to a discussion of Character-Based Leadership, the topic of personal integrity is fundamental. On its most simplistic level, integrity can be reduced to the question: Is what you do consistent with what you say? This is often referred to as "walking your talk." From the point of view of evaluating our own integrity or the integrity of others, this is perhaps the best test, yet whether you walk your talk is far more complex and more challenging to do than this simple question may imply.

Consider this excerpt from the *Stanford Encyclopedia of Philosophy (1987)*:

> A person of integrity is willing to bear the consequences of her convictions, even when this is difficult... A person whose only principle is "Seek my own pleasure" is not a candidate for integrity because there is no possibility of conflict—between pleasure and principle—in which integrity could be lost. Where there is no possibility of its loss, integrity cannot exist. Similarly in the case of the approval seeker. The single-minded pursuit of approval is inconsistent with integrity... A commitment to spinelessness does not vitiate its spinelessness—another of integrity's contraries. The same may be said for the ruthless seeker of wealth. A person whose only aim is to increase his bank balance is a person for whom nothing is ruled out: duplicity, theft, murder. Expedience is *contrasted* to a life of principle, so an ascription of integrity is out of place. Like the

pleasure seeker and the approval seeker, he lacks a "core," the kind of commitments that give a person character and that make a loss of integrity possible. In order to sell one's soul, one must have something to sell.

Walking your talk with rigor and consistency is difficult work, even for the most seasoned of leaders. It requires that you speak both mindfully and purposefully. It also requires that you both face and make tough choices; choices that are sometimes painful for you and perhaps also for others. As a leader, the consistency with which you walk your talk is the basis on which others will choose whether to follow your lead. This makes building the foundation for your integrity essential to your leadership.

Personal integrity is fundamental to your leadership as someone who is committed to Character-Based Leadership. Your integrity, or lack thereof, will define you, and it will define your leadership whether you bring consciousness to it or not. By exploring the distinct facets of your personal integrity, you will have access to establishing a stronger foundation for your leadership. You could say this exploration is a conscious effort to define what character, specifically your character, means to you. This foundation is not something that can be defined for you or given to you by others. You must design and build the foundation for yourself.

If you already consider yourself to be a person of high integrity, the clarity you can gain from this exploration can help you to grow to a whole new level. It can also help you to cultivate leadership in others. If integrity is something that has been challenging for you in some way, this exploration can support you in establishing the foundation you need to become the kind of leader you want to be.

Introducing the Essential Dimensions of Personal Integrity

There are two essential dimensions of personal integrity that I suggest you consider when building your foundation: *authenticity* and *accountability*. With a new level of clarity and specificity, you will be better able to align your words and your actions, make difficult decisions with more certainty and confidence, and more easily observe when you are out of alignment. This clarity will also help you to more easily see how to correct course.

The first dimension to consider is *authenticity*, which is about being sincere in your commitments and intentions. To be authentic, you must first know what those commitments and intentions are, not as an expectation from the outside, but rather as a personal declaration of your values, principles and commitments. When you are being authentic, your words and actions are aligned with each other, i.e., you walk your talk. In addition, both your words and actions are aligned with your beliefs and commitments. Authenticity requires that you are true to yourself.

The second dimension to consider is *accountability*. To be accountable is to be willing to make a promise to another with a commitment to honoring that promise. It is about being true to your word by doing what you say you will do. Even when you fail to deliver as promised for any reason, you remain true by owning and taking responsibility for the consequences and your relationships. Accountability requires that we are dedicated to our commitments to others.

Authenticity

At its most basic level, personal integrity is about being true to our personal beliefs, values and principles. It is the source of our personal power and of our credibility in the world. By "true," I mean "a constant and loyal adherence to" as opposed to a moral judgment that ascribes right and wrong.

This distinction between personal truth and morality is important in the discussion of integrity as it applies to Character-Based Leadership because integrity is a very personal matter. Although it is likely that those who are reading this share a similar moral code, the subject of integrity is not inherently about our particular interpretations of morality.

From the point of view of Character-Based Leadership, the discussion of integrity begins with a personal inquiry into what values and principles each of us will use as the guide for choosing our words and our actions. You could call this your personal code of ethics. While your foundational values and principles are likely to be influenced by your family, culture and religion, you ultimately get to choose the values and principles by which you will live.

Consider that choosing your values and principles rather than mindlessly inheriting them can make the difference between consciously building a strong and enduring foundation of integrity from the inside out and embarking on a never-ending quest to live up to someone else's standards.

The former will be a great source of your personal power and influence. The more consciously you choose, the more naturally your words and deeds will be aligned and the more aware you will be when you are faced with situations that challenge your personal code of ethics. The latter is likely to leave a wake of guilt, shame and blame, for that is the cost of any attempt to stay true to ethical and moral standards or expectations to which you have not or cannot authentically commit.

> *Choosing to do the right thing because doing the wrong thing would make you look bad is an act of manipulation, not integrity.*

Though your integrity manifests in the outer world via your words and deeds, it is entirely an inner game for you to master. Mindfully choosing the values and principles that will guide your words, actions and decisions is an essential step in developing yourself as a Character-Based Leader.

Here are a few words of caution:

- Choosing and living from your values and principles has nothing to do with fulfilling the expectations of others. The most important judge of your authenticity will ultimately be you.
- Living in personal integrity does not make you better than or superior to others. It does fortify your character, thereby making you stronger personally and more able to lead others effectively. It also enables you to fulfill your potential and empowers you to make the biggest possible difference you can make in the world.

Choosing to do the right thing because doing the wrong thing would make you look bad is an act of manipulation, not integrity. T. Harv Ecker, author of *Secrets of the Millionaire Mind*, has a saying: "How you do one thing is how you do everything." What you do when no one is looking is more telling of your true character and real motivations than what you do when others are watching.

Your strength as a Character-Based Leader begins with your authenticity. You are strengthened every time you speak and act in alignment with your chosen values and principles, your personal code of ethics. You cannot possibly be authentic consistently if you are not crystal clear about what authenticity means to you.

There are many processes available for defining your values and guiding principles. Since these values and principles are the foundation for your integrity, I offer a process here to guide you. Regardless of the process you use, it is critical to your development as a Character-Based Leader to do this work. Your personal code of ethics is the core of the foundation for your integrity. Clarity about what is authentic for you at the level of values and principles facilitates consistency in thought, word and deed.

A Simple Process for Defining Your Values and Guiding Principles

I. **Draft Your Values and Guiding Principles**
   a. **Explore What Your Values and Guiding Principles Could Be**
      i. **What 5 words represent your core values?** A core value is an important and enduring belief or ideal that must be met for you to experience being on solid ground. One way to know that a value is core is when you feel a significant emotional charge when that value is not satisfied in the words, choices or actions of yourself or others.

      Some examples of words that represent my personal values are compassion, innovation, freedom, curiosity, justice, sustainability and empowerment. To come up with your words, consider what really matters to you. If you had to describe who you were to someone else, what words would you use to describe yourself?

      ii. **What are the principles that guide you in your choices and behavior?** A guiding principle is any principle or precept that guides your choices and behavior throughout your life in all circumstances, irrespective of changes in *goals, strategies, type of work, position,* and so on.

Some examples are: Do the right thing. Look and listen for the gold in people. Never stop learning. Take personal responsibility—I always have a choice.

b. Explore What Your Values and Guiding Principles Have Been

Note: Feel free to use something you have already created for yourself. Whatever work you have already done on your values and guiding principles will be very useful here.

i. Write about a time when you made a difficult decision and were satisfied that you made the right choice.
    1. Describe the internal conflict(s) you had to work through to make that decision. These conflicts could be, for example, (1) between what would have been comfortable for you to do versus what you thought was the right thing to do; (2) between your commitments and your personal wants and/or needs; (3) between agendas, such as your personal agenda and the agenda of a group to which you belong; (4) between competing priorities; or (5) between competing values.
    2. Read what you wrote. Now write down the values and principles from the story that guided your decision.

ii. Write about a time when you made what you felt, in hindsight, was the wrong decision.
    1. Read what you wrote. Now write down what values and principles you hold that makes it seem like the wrong decision to you now. If it's helpful, consider the examples of possible internal conflicts to help you distinguish the values and principles that are the source of your assessment.

iii. Write about a time you took an action that was clearly outside of what you normally would do and/or outside of your comfort zone.
    1. What compelled you to take such a bold action?
    2. What was the risk of the action you took?
    3. Why at the time did it seem like it was worth the risk?

        4.   What happened as a result? What difference did you make?

        5.   In hindsight, was it worth it? Why or why not?

iv.   Continue to write stories and to identify the values and guiding principles until you are satisfied that you have identified your core values and principles. A good rule of thumb is to find five to seven principles and three to five values. You already have been guided by values and principles whether or not you have been conscious of them or have written them down. The point of this part of the exercise is to distinguish what your guiding values and principles have been to this point.

II. Craft What Your Values and Guiding Principles Could Be

a. Your Values

   i.   Take out a fresh piece of paper and write the values you distinguished on a single page, leaving at least three lines between each.

   ii.   Write a one-line statement of what each value means to you.

   iii. Are any of your values similar enough that they could be represented by a single value? If so, select the value that best represents the core idea, then make sure the one-line description is sufficient to capture the core idea and the nuances of the values you combined. Cross out the values you combined into the one representing the core idea. See if you can reduce your list to no more than five values.

   iv. Once you have refined your list, is there anything missing that you think must be included to say your values are complete? If so, add it.

b. Your Principles

   i.   Take out a fresh piece of paper and write the principles you distinguished on a single page, leaving at least three lines between each.

   ii.   Are any of these principles similar? If so, choose the one that best represents the core idea of those that are similar and write the aspects that may be missing from the one you chose in the space you allotted beneath the principle. Then cross off the ones that you have combined. See if you can reduce this list to seven principles.

      iii.   Once you have refined your list, is there anything missing that you think must be included to say your principles are complete?

III. Choose What Your Values and Guiding Principles Will Be

Now that you have identified and crafted the language of your core values and guiding principles, it is time to choose.

Clarity is power. The ultimate sign that you are ready to make this choice is that you are excited about your level of clarity and feel certain that what you have crafted represents who you are and what you believe. Now you may also be a bit nervous because choosing to live by what you have written is likely a tall order, even if many of these values and guiding principles have already been guiding you and your integrity is already strong.

By choosing, you are declaring to yourself, "These are my values and guiding principles," and you are making the following promise to yourself: "From this moment forward, I will choose my words and actions, and make decisions that are consistently true to these in all of my endeavors."

If you are serious about developing your personal integrity to the next level, then clarifying your values and guiding principles is critically important. If you aren't feeling at least some sense of excitement or nervousness about what you have crafted and about making the choice to live by them, you are probably not done working on them. If you are having trouble getting to a place of clarity, satisfaction or excitement about your values and principles, I encourage you to get assistance from someone who understands the importance and who has skill in this arena.

Whatever you do, *do not* skip over this step of consciously choosing. "I'll try" or "I'll do my best" is not a sufficient level of commitment to build a foundation for developing your personal integrity as an individual or as a leader of others.

IV. Declare Your Personal Code of Ethics

With clear values and principles to ensure that your thoughts, words and deeds are consistently aligned, you are better equipped to consistently be authentic and walk your talk.

Authenticity is first and foremost a promise you make to yourself. You can also declare your personal code of ethics to others. By doing so, you make it clear to others what they can expect from you. This accomplishes two things. The first is that you are setting the expectations for what is authentic for you rather than relying on others' interpretations of what should be authentic for you. The second is that you are inviting others to hold you accountable. We are sometimes blind to how our words and actions appear to others. Feedback ensures that our interpretation of our authenticity matches what others see and experience. When you are leading others, this feedback is critical to your learning and development.

Declaring your personal code of ethics to others should not be done lightly. Do this only if you are truly committed to following through with consistency and if you are willing to be held accountable. A sustained commitment to being consistent in applying your personal code of ethics is essential to your integrity, both in terms of how you experience it and how others experience and judge you. If others have an interpretation that you do not walk your talk, it does not really matter if you think they are wrong; it means there is something for you to learn about yourself and about integrity. By seeking to understand the perceptions of others, you will discover your blind spots and improve the perception of your integrity in the world. The ultimate payoff of this will be an increase in trust, respect and, ultimately, influence.

Accountability

The moment you declare any commitment to another, as when you declare your personal code of ethics, you are consciously entering into an accountable relationship. While accountability is often discussed in the context of managing work and activities, it is actually about managing your relationship with integrity.

Authenticity is essentially about walking your talk by ensuring that your values, principles, words and actions are in alignment as experienced by you and perceived by others. Being authentic requires that you consistently align your thoughts with your words and actions. It is the inner game of integrity. Accountability is about being true to your word by making promises to others and honoring those promises; it is how you bring integrity to your relationships. Accountability is the transactional level of living a life of integrity. Even in the absence of having clear values and guiding principles, you can go to work on building your integrity in every relationship and every interaction by learning the principles and practices of accountability.

Before going any further, it is important that we distinguish between personal responsibility and accountability. These terms are often used interchangeably, which can cause confusion. Personal responsibility is about your relationship with yourself and the circumstances of your life. When you are personally responsible, you think and act from the point of view that everything you are, everything you do, and everything you have is up to you. *QBQ! The Question behind the Question* by John G. Miller contains a clever rephrasing of the Serenity Prayer that captures an important aspect of personal responsibility: "Grant me the serenity to accept the people I cannot change, change the ones I can, and the wisdom to know the only one I can change is me."

Whereas personal responsibility is about your relationship with yourself and the circumstances of your life, accountability is about your relationship with others and with your word. As defined earlier, to be accountable means to be willing to make a promise with a commitment to honoring that promise. Every time we make promises to others, we can expect that they will ultimately make assessments about both our personal integrity and our relationship with them. The two are inextricably linked.

You may have noticed that making a promise and honoring that promise are distinct in this definition of accountability. Both are required to create a relationship with integrity, but they are two very specific domains of action. By understanding the dimensions of both domains of action, you will see opportunities to improve the integrity of your relationships.

The Practice of Making Clear and Specific Promises

A promise is a commitment by someone to do (or not do) something. Specificity is key to accountability. People often talk about the need to manage expectations, particularly as it applies to work relationships. Consider this: In accountable relationships, there are no expectations; there are clearly negotiated agreements. In the absence of doing the work to form clear agreements, you leave integrity up to the whim of expectations that are all too often moving targets.

By ensuring that you form agreements that include, at a minimum, the essential elements described below, you increase the likelihood of both a satisfying outcome for all involved and an increase in trust in the relationship. This is a very specific way you can take personal responsibility for the integrity of your relationships as well as for your personal integrity. In contrast, failing to form such agreements puts both your integrity and your relationships at risk.

There are two considerations that most often get in the way of being rigorous in negotiating clear agreements. The first is time. Being rigorous in negotiating clear agreements absolutely can take more time than not doing so, especially when you are learning to be more specific. Yet consider the cost when there are misunderstandings and unmet expectations. Not only does it cost you potentially far more time to clean up the mess of misinterpretation, but it can cost you something far more valuable—trust.

The second is some version of "we know each other well enough, so it's not necessary" or "it will all work out." My view is that assuming anything when it comes to communication between people is risky. In the absence of clarity, there is room for interpretation, and when there is room for interpretation, there is likely to be misinterpretation. Once again, is it worth the risk?

The essential elements of a promise answer these questions:

1. What? Any relevant specifics about the features and facts of what is being promised.
2. By when? A specific date and possibly time.
3. What are the conditions of satisfaction? The Business Dictionary (businessdictionary.com) offers this definition: "Criteria by which the outcome of a contract, program, or project may be

measured." When it comes to creating accountable relationships, conditions of satisfaction are more specifically the criteria that define a shared interpretation of success and mutual satisfaction.

These elements are not rocket science. Being rigorous is simple, although it is not always easy. It takes practice and commitment. Consider though that your integrity is a function of how rigorous you are willing to be in every conversation you have. If you are committed to your integrity, there is only one choice to make: Do the hard work to ensure that your relationships work.

Honoring Your Promises

Notice this does not say "keeping your promises." I would venture to say that there is not a person alive that has kept every promise he or she has made. There are times when, no matter how committed you are and no matter how hard you try, you will fail to keep a promise. The difference between someone who is accountable and someone who is not lies in what they do when things break down. Let's take a look at what honoring a promise is and is not as a way to distinguish what you need to do to be accountable when failure to keep a promise is imminent.

Honoring a promise *is*:

1. notifying the person to whom you made a promise as soon as you see that you may not be able to keep your promise so you can together anticipate the breakdown and take appropriate action.
2. revoking a promise you made when you see that you cannot keep it and supporting the person making the original request in finding an alternative to get what he or she needs.
3. acknowledging when you fail to deliver in any aspect of the promise you made and taking personal responsibility for dealing with the consequences in terms of your relationship and in terms of the breakdown that may have been caused for others.
4. renegotiating when you discover that you cannot deliver what you originally promised in any respect with a commitment to ensure that both of you are satisfied even if the terms of your agreement change.

Honoring a promise is *not*:

1. giving a good reason for why you did not keep a promise (Your reason may be valid and perfectly understandable, but be mindful of using your reason as an excuse to get yourself off the hook for the breakdown rather than taking personal responsibility for the effect of your failure to keep your promise.)
2. telling someone after the fact that you are sorry you didn't do what you said you would.
3. waiting for the person to whom you made the promise to come to you, assuming that if they don't, it wasn't that important.

You can see from these examples that you can honor your promises even when you fail to deliver as promised. To be accountable requires that you remain true in your commitments to others. This does not mean you need to be perfect. You can remain true to your commitments by either keeping your promise or by owning and taking responsibility for both the consequences and your relationships when you cannot or do not remain true to the commitment for whatever reason.

Honoring your commitments can be very hard, especially in a time of great change and seemingly ever-growing expectation for us to do more. There are times when you may do one or all of the things listed under "Honoring your promises is *not*." What I am suggesting could be considered an uncommonly high standard for integrity and accountability in the world today. The point is not to use this as a framework from which to judge yourself or others, but rather a standard of conduct to aspire to in everything you do. By holding yourself to a standard higher than the norm, you will begin to naturally raise the standards of others around you. If you

Holding yourself and others to a higher level of integrity is not about judgment or punishment.

are not already known for having impeccable integrity when it comes to doing what you say you will do, you can quickly develop a reputation as someone who can be counted on. The possible rewards include increased trust and respect from others and of others, more influence, and possibly even bigger opportunities. Perhaps most importantly, you will likely experience an increase in trust and confidence in yourself and others.

Holding yourself and others to a higher level of integrity is not about judgment or punishment. The most empowering context for holding someone to account is a commitment for yourself and others to be and do their absolute best. Any failure to do so is an opportunity to learn, to grow, and to correct course rather than to blame, shame or punish. When we punish others or ourselves for not living up to a high standard, we are more likely to shrink the commitments we are willing to make either in terms of magnitude or multitude to protect ourselves rather than to seize the opportunity to learn, to grow, and to aspire to be and do more.

Why Choose to Raise the Bar on Your Integrity?

According to Wikipedia, integrity "comprises the personal inner sense of wholeness deriving from honesty and consistent uprightness of character." That definition comes from the etymological origins of the word "integrity." Integrity derives from "integer," the Latin word for "whole."

That "personal inner sense of wholeness derived from honesty and uprightness of character" includes being authentic, as in living true to your beliefs, values and principles, as well as being accountable in your relationships with others. We feel good about ourselves and experience being centered when we act with integrity in this sense, yet we also experience that "personal inner sense of wholeness" from pursuing our passions and purposes. This includes things like doing what we love to do, pursuing causes or purposes that matter to us, and using the best of our talents and skills to make a difference. In fact, while in pursuit of things that truly matter to us, we are more likely to be willing to endure the pain of the tough decisions. When we are doing what we love, aligning our walk with our talk can be more of a natural expression than a Herculean effort. When pursuing our dreams, we are more apt to lead. We are more likely called to take a strong stand and to make bigger and bolder promises for something beyond the ordinary, even when everyone around us seems to be arguing for the status quo.

Living a life of integrity is a promise to yourself that you will do the right thing according to your values and principles, and that you will be accountable to others. You can be an individual of high integrity by consistently making choices that are in alignment with your values and principles and honoring your promises to others. Integrity, by its very nature, requires us to opt for what is often the harder choice. Living at this level of integrity is a choice to lead yourself and perhaps even others purely by your example. Imagine what the world would be like if more people made that choice. Yet if you want to be a leader for the sake of something bigger than you, your foundation must be designed accordingly.

As leaders in the world, passion and purpose are your "why," the reason you are willing to make those difficult choices over and over and the reason you are willing to hold yourself to a higher standard. When you are leading from your passion and purpose, you are also more likely to be influential in the world. The more grounded you are in your "why," the less likely you are to focus on your own discomfort or fear in making and keeping promises. You are also less likely to succumb to the temptation to let those fears drive your choices rather than your values, principles and commitments.

When you have a clear "why" based on your passion and purpose, when the going gets tough you are likely to remain more focused on the future that you are committed to realizing and the difference you are making than to focus on the pain and challenge of the moment.

In short, the bigger your commitments in the world, the less your decisions of personal integrity are about you.

The questions for reflection below are intended only to begin your inquiry into your "why." Why is it worth holding yourself to an even higher standard of integrity? I highly recommend that you take the time to do further work in this area. The assessments below are sufficient for a strong start in further developing your personal integrity. Your responses will connect you with what you care most about and will support you in thinking about your reason for working on your personal integrity.

Integrity Is Not about Perfection

The rigor and consistency with which you walk your talk and are true to your word are essential to your integrity, but keep in mind that living and leading with integrity is an aspirational way of life. Success does not equal perfection, nor is there a goal of perfection. The strengthening of your foundation happens over time and requires both commitment and practice.

A strong foundation of integrity requires a commitment to the practice of being true to your values, your principles and yourself. It is a promise to be the best *you* possible, to mindfully practice a rigorous adherence to your values and principles in your words and deeds, and to be consistent in doing so.

If you are human, you will make mistakes. In the context of integrity, a mistake is choosing words or actions that are in violation of your chosen values and principles or failing to honor a promise. If you aspire to live and lead with integrity and you misstep, your focus will be on owning your mistake, addressing the consequences, and taking the action necessary to restore your integrity with yourself and others.

The Power of Observation

There is no judgment in practice. There is only observation, learning and a commitment to apply what you learn. Adopting this perspective gives you permission to be human and empowers you to see and embrace every misstep as an opportunity to learn and grow.

Observation is essential to improving your practice, so learning to recognize and use feedback from the world around you is a critical aspect of strengthening your foundation over time. The people, events and circumstances of your life provide a mirror of sorts through which to observe your rigor and consistency in your practices around integrity.

As part of exploring authenticity as a dimension of your personal integrity, you crafted and chose values and guiding principles to use as the basis for choosing your words and actions and for making decisions. The next challenge is to invent and discover ways to ensure that you apply them rigorously and consistently in everything you do from this point forward. Regardless of your level of clarity, demonstrated rigor and consistency, I suggest that you include periodic assessment as a practice. Following is a suggestion for how to approach your assessment. There is no right way to do this. The point is to get the feedback you need to ensure that you continue to learn and grow.

I. Self Assessment: Getting a Sense of How Well You Are Doing

If you want to assess your progress, it is a good idea to know where you are starting from. Every time you perform this assessment, and I suggest you do it at least quarterly, it is an opportunity to bring your values and guiding principles back into full focus.

    a.   Take out a clean copy of your chosen values. For each value, using a scale of 1–10 (1 = not at all, 5 = half the time, 10 = always), rate how well you think you are living true to each value. Write the number next to the value and write down the reason for your rating.

    b.   Take out a clean copy of your chosen guiding principles. For each principle, using a scale of 1–10 (1 = not at all, 5 = half the time, 10 = always), rate how well you think you are living true to this principle. Write the number next to the value and write down the reason for your rating.

II. Partner Assessment: Getting Feedback from Others

I specifically use the term *partner* here because it is important to choose people who are committed to your success and willing to support you in your commitment to developing your personal integrity. You want people who will be honest with you and whose opinion and perspective you both value and trust.

Identify three to five people you consider to be your partner as explained above. Request that they meet with you for half an hour to provide you with the feedback you are requesting. Send them the following instructions in your own words three days prior to your meeting:

- This should take no more than 15 minutes to complete.
- Please be completely honest. The more honest you are, the more useful your assessment will be.
- Bring your completed assessment to our meeting on _____.
- Thank you for taking the time to support me!

    a.   Page 1: For each value, using a scale of 1–10 (1 = not at all, 5 = half the time, 10 = always), rate how well you think I am living true to this value. Write the number next to the value and write down the reason for your rating. Go with your gut.

b. Page 2: For each guiding principle, using a scale of 1–10 (1 = not at all, 5 = half the time, 10 = always), rate how well you think I am living true to this principle. Write the number next to the value and write down the reason for your rating.

III. Applying Your Values and Guiding Principles in Everyday Life

Living true to your values and guiding principles doesn't have an action plan. It is not something you add to your to-do list. Integrity is not something you do, but rather it is the context for everything you do. Your values and guiding principles, as well as a commitment to being accountable, are your chosen standard for your personal integrity. These are your truing mechanism.

The key to success is to find a way to make your foundation for your personal integrity an integral part of the way you think in everyday life. First and foremost, you must keep the foundation present. In the beginning, it may seem like a lot to remember. Do not try to remember anything. Consciously apply it often instead and this foundation won't just be something you remember, but will become the source of how you think, what you say, and what you do.

In the beginning, it is essential to keep a copy of your values and guiding principles with you at all times. Put it on the wall in your office. Print it on a business card, laminate it, and put it in your wallet. Turn it into a screen saver on your computer, smart phone or tablet. Put it where you can access it and use it every day in some way. The more you use it, the less you will find you have to refer to it. Any time you communicate or need to make a decision is an opportunity to apply it.

Although assessments are a helpful technique, they are not the ultimate measure for your growth and development in the arena of your personal integrity. The purpose of crafting and choosing your values and guiding principles is to lead yourself and others with a new level of clarity and specificity. The ultimate indicator is in your response to these questions:

1. Are you better able to align your words and your actions?
2. Are you making difficult decisions with more certainty and confidence?

3. Are you able to observe when your words, actions or decisions are out of alignment with your values and principles?
4. Are you more skilled in correcting course when you observe that you have not acted with integrity?
5. Are the people who are counting on you as well as those you lead saying in their own way that you walk your talk?

A yes or no response is only a small part of answering these questions. I encourage you to take the time to consider examples for your response to every one of these questions. Every time you make an assessment or answer these questions fully is an opportunity to learn to strengthen the soundness of the foundation for your personal integrity.

Your personal integrity is the source of your strength as a Character-Based Leader. By fortifying your foundation with these principles and practices, you will grow stronger every day. Enjoy the journey as you build and reinforce this critical aspect of your leadership. And remember to acknowledge and celebrate your accomplishments every step of the way.

Chapter 12

Real Leadership:
The Power of Humility

S. Max Brown

"Daddy, put your phone away," begged my daughter. Though I had promised to go out and play with her, I found myself pulled away by e-mail that was consuming our time together, and she

Humility isn't timidity or weakness. It is confidence, wisdom, and grace combined with an acknowledgment that we are all imperfect.

was understandably frustrated with the delay. "Daddy, put it away so we can play," she pleaded after patiently waiting for several minutes.

"Daddy, please put it away," she pleaded for the third time as she positioned herself right in front of me. I finally relented, and she promptly thanked me for listening. Once again, I had let my own inflated sense of self-importance rise above the needs of my family and my promise to be present. While we had a great afternoon playing together, I quietly pondered what would have happened if my daughter hadn't been so persistent. How many times have I let my ego take over and thus disappointed someone who wasn't as persistent as my daughter was that day? Sure, it may have seemed like a simple thing, but what if I had broken my promise? How does self-centeredness affect our lives? How would it have affected my relationship with my daughter?

Research done by Doctors Jean Twenge and Keith Campbell suggests that the rise in narcissism (the overinflated ego) is destroying community and relationships. In fact, arrogant people are proud to identify how great they are, but often feel less empathetic or understanding toward others. This is not the act of ignoring others, but rather a blatant inability to care.

The pitfalls of arrogant behavior often happen in subtle ways. Most recently, scientists have confirmed that narcissistic leaders reduce the information flow between team members, directly contributing to poor team performance. Often, team members don't realize that a narcissistic leader is a problem until it is too late.

Nothing derails a leader, a business initiative, a relationship, or even a noble cause faster than an overinflated ego, yet we often go to work without a thought for the actual costs of arrogance. We, and our organizations, reward those who are overly confident, while never stopping to calculate the liability or opportunities lost because of such arrogance. Even worse, we frequently suffer from blind spots that subtlety trick us into believing that ego is someone else's problem. Imagine how much more productive we could be with a little humility.

Humility is one of the most critical, yet often overlooked and misunderstood, virtues of great leadership. Despite decades of research to support the importance of it, many still discount the need to practice it. Perhaps it is because humility has suffered from a perception problem; viewed as a weakness or a vulnerability that can be trampled on by others. However, this perspective is wrong. Humility isn't timidity or weakness. It is confidence, wisdom, and grace combined with an acknowledgment that we are all imperfect.

"As a trait, humility is the point of equilibrium between too much ego and not enough. Humility provides the crucial balance between the two extremes," declare David Marcum and Steven Smith in their book titled *Egonomics*. Indeed, humility is the ability to be happy with who we are, and the realization that we're still incomplete.

So how do we stay grounded? How do we keep this balance? How do we obtain humility? Don't dismiss the forthcoming answer due to the simplicity of the statement, but rather consider the implications of these two words: Serve others.

Real leadership is about helping those around us become successful. Neuroscience confirms that happiness and engagement are higher in people who are focused on others. Indeed, when we serve others, we become more connected and enjoy stronger social support.

Humility is the ability to recognize that we are better together. As we become more aware of those around us, our own needs actually begin to overlap with others' in a united effort toward mutual success. Instead of viewing the time spent playing with my daughter as a chore, I realigned my own definition of success to remember that family relationships are a critical source of happiness in my own life. I'm grateful for a daughter who persistently and patiently reminded me of this priority.

Imagine how much more productive we all could be with a little more humility.

Chapter 13

Leading Yourself into Humility

Dan Rockwell

How many ways can you complete the statement "I can usually tell if young leaders have the [blank] to make it?"

Back on the farm, the first thing my dad said about someone he admired was "They're smart." I grew up admiring smart. I could fill in the blank "I can usually tell if young leaders have the brains to make it." Surprisingly, leadership isn't about superior intellect. During a presentation at the World Business Forum 2011, Harvard professor and author Bill George said, "Once you get to an IQ of 120, intelligence isn't a major factor in leadership success."

You might complete the sentence "I can usually tell if young leaders have the talent to make it." But, we've all seen talented people crash and burn, which leads me to say you could complete the sentence with "discipline" or "self-control" because talent without discipline is missed potential.

How about filling the blank in with courage, vision, passion, drive, initiative, honesty or education?

G. J. Hart, CEO of Texas Roadhouse, who leads more than 40,000 employees, surprised me by the way he filled in the blank. I was fortunate to spend an hour talking with him in March of 2011. I'll never forget G. J.'s comment regarding high-potential leaders. "I can usually tell if they have the *humility* to make it." For G. J., humility said it all.

Intelligence, talent, courage, vision or any other leadership quality you can list fails without humility. Talents and intelligence have limitations. Your talent in one area exposes lack of talent in another.

Humility always applies, regardless. Simply put, humility yields success; arrogance blocks it.

Thinking we know too much blocks knowledge. When we think we already know, we don't think we need to learn. In contrast, humility welcomes knowledge. Sadly, the things we *think* we know block the things we *should* know, like the value of lifting others, stepping aside so others can shine, and taking the blame while giving the credit.

How do we lead ourselves into humility?

There's something that matters more than knowing. Goethe said, "Knowing is not enough; we must apply. Willing is not enough; we must do." Putting theory into practice challenges, reveals and establishes true knowledge. You've heard newly married couples bragging about how their marriage is going to be different. You've heard inexperienced leaders proudly explaining the "right" path. "If I was in charge, things would be different," some people say. For those who haven't performed, the path is clear.

Practice helps produce humility. Doing explodes the myth of perceived competence. I used to teach computer classes. Students casually listened to me explain how to copy and paste, something we all know today. I could see the look of confidence in their eyes as if hearing me say it and knowing about the copy and paste functions were the same as knowing how to do them. I burst their bubble of perceived competence by saying, "Go ahead and do it on your own." At that point, they were ready to really listen, and they were humble.

Humility can be learned, but not in theory, only in practice. I believe we can teach ourselves humility. Thomas Watson said, "Nothing so conclusively proves a man's ability to lead others as what he does from day to day to lead himself." Your leadership success depends on your ability to lead yourself into the essential quality of humility.

Humility is an attitude, but more importantly, it's a practice. I'll acknowledge that we can be proud of our humility and, in so doing, defeat the process. We can act humbly while being filled with arrogance. Even so, the practice is worth it. Humility, like all the other things in life that matter, is a journey. Practice it even when you don't feel it.

Let's focus on seven practices you can employ to lead yourself into humility by examining things that humble people do.

1. ***Restore broken relationships.***

Few things are more humbling than taking responsibility for your part in a broken relationship. Not long ago, a friend I'd grown distant from said, "Dan, I never came to you because I thought you had your mind made up." I felt like saying that's lame. But as you can tell, my direct approach can be off-putting and was the reason he hadn't said anything in the first place. I took a breath and said, "I was wrong for coming across in ways that closed you out. I apologize."

I don't feel good telling you this story. It's humbling. My pride tells me to make myself look good by blaming others. Few things are more humbling than taking responsibility for one's part in an argument or broken relationship, but doing so is one way to lead yourself into humility.

2. ***Treat others better than you treat yourself.***

Boy, that one feels like sand in the underwear. I have a little balancing scale in my head. It compares the good others have done for me with the good I've done for them. I like to keep it even. I don't want you to give me too much because it makes me feel obligated. I know, that's my problem. But I don't want to give you too much, either; it makes me feel used.

Humility destroys the scales. I'm not talking about enabling users, that's not good for anyone. I'm talking about serving others without expecting a return. When you feel the scales telling you someone owes you, ignore them. The scales are bondage. When you start feeling someone owes you, serve them again. I think it's freeing to lead ourselves into this expression of humility.

3. ***Acknowledge weaknesses and embrace strengths.***

Practice these together. Acknowledging weaknesses is only one side of leading yourself into humility; the other is finding comfort with your strengths.

In a strange way, the ability to embrace your strengths is humble. Humble people don't deny reality. When I see someone who can't take a compliment, who is reluctant to acknowledge their abilities, I don't think of them as humble; I think of the person as weak, unconfident or perhaps secretly arrogant and waiting for someone to tell them they do have strengths.

It's odd that reluctance to embrace our strengths is actually subtle arrogance. This reluctance says, "Focus on me; lift me." In contrast, the ability to graciously accept a compliment is a sign of humility. I'll never forget the time a person I admired complimented me on my sense of style. I'm still embarrassed by the lesson I gave him on how I chose my clothing. I know now that it was arrogance that motivated my response.

You can lead yourself into humility by saying "thank you" when someone compliments you and leaving it at that.

4. Thank others for support and encouragement.

Gratitude tempers arrogance. No one is an island. Any success you've attained involves others. The greater your success, the more others are involved. You can lead yourself into humility by constantly thinking about and publicly acknowledging the people who lifted you.

5. Let others perform while you observe and encourage.

I'm all about developing emerging leaders. That means I frequently lead from the back while they stretch their leadership muscles. This habit didn't come naturally, but I'm learning to let others get the credit for things we developed together.

Here's a subtle way arrogance leaks out: after an emerging leader performs, giving them insignificant criticism. Tweaking is arrogance. If it's not significant, don't say it. Lead yourself into humility by observing and encouraging rather than observing and tweaking.

6. Ask dumb questions.

Mike Howard, Chief Security Officer at Microsoft, got me thinking about this one. During our interview, he said that getting over the fear of asking dumb questions was an important growth point in his leadership. A know-it-all is arrogant. Humility is openness; arrogance is blindness. The path to wisdom is paved with humility. When you stop pretending you know something, you become able to know.

I just finished reading Pat Lencioni's book *Getting Naked*. He echoes the same idea. If you have a dumb question, it's likely that others have it too. Pride keeps us from asking; humility is willing to be embarrassed. Additionally, from a leadership perspective, being dumb up front is better than being dumb in the end.

7. Delight in rich, sustaining relationships.

Arrogance yields agonizing emptiness. Humility welcomes others. Few things are more useful to the practice of humility than rich relationships in which friends speak the truth, even when it hurts. Bob Hancox has been coaching me for the past few months. During that time, I've come to see that I keep people at arm's length. Vulnerability isn't my thing. I'm learning to let the inner me out, the one I protect because I don't want to get hurt.

Bob helped me see that the reason I didn't have more rich relationships is me, not others. Ouch! It's part of the practice of humility.

No one can humble you. Only you can humble you. Only you can lead yourself into humility. You've seen haughty people remain arrogant when they should act humbly. Forced humility actually breaks your spirit. On the other hand, embracing humility frees and energizes you. Only you can lead yourself into humility by practicing it.

> *When you stop pretending you know something, you become able to know.*

Granted, pursuing humility is slippery and perilous because we can become proud that we are working on humility, and we can become proud of our humility. Additionally, comparing ourselves with others may result in self-congratulation. We can always find someone worse than we are.

Arrogant people are self-justifying. They don't grow and learn. Just like with the students in those early computer classes, practice helps burst the bubble of perceived competence. When you stop talking about humility and start practicing humility, you are leading yourself into the central component of Character-Based Leadership. G. J. Hart showed me the conundrum that arrogance is weakness and humility is strength. It opens doors to our highest potential and builds foundations for rich leadership.

Chapter 14

The Noble Choice

Chad Balthrop

On the surface, it seems strange to write an article about the virtue of humility and how one can grow in it. Our current understanding might suggest that the more we think we have learned humility, the less truly humble we have become. It's not lost on me that anyone arrogant enough to think he could author the definitive, step-by-step formula for becoming humble can't possibly have a clue about the topic at hand. I was tempted to name this chapter "Humility and How I Achieved It." After all, I thought I was conceited until I found out I was perfect.

All kidding aside, the very act of considering a topic as significant and counterintuitive as humility is a humbling exercise in self-examination. I can't claim to be an expert on humility. Neither can I share with you insight gained from my profound experience of becoming a humble person. What I can do is speak as an adoring fan and devoted admirer. Like a young boy who has memorized all the stats on his favorite baseball player and favorite team, I can recount to you the common characteristics of those who are champions in the world of humility. We can discover ways to follow in their footsteps and learn from their examples. Perhaps someday, if we watch closely enough and practice long enough, we can become examples for someone else.

What Is Humility?

From our first steps together, I must acknowledge that John Dickson's book, *HUMILITAS, A Lost Key to Life, Love and Leadership*, has greatly influenced my thoughts on humility and my comments here. His historical analysis of the contrast between our modern view of humility and that of ancient cultures highlights a subtle yet profound truth: There is a difference between the virtue of humility and an act of humiliation.

A strong and natural aversion to humiliation causes most people to avoid any attempt to grow in the virtue of humility. In relation to leadership, humility is even further misunderstood. Leadership comes in a variety of flavors.

Positional leaders often maintain influence by virtue of the position they hold. Positional leaders can be benevolent or malevolent. The influence they exert is directly tied to the authority associated with their titles or stations. Being humble in the presence of positional leaders makes logical sense; we bow before the king because the king can have us killed. That act of submission is not humility at work but rather the humiliation associated with being "beneath" someone in authority over us.

In ancient writings, this is almost exclusively the form of humility described. Humility before one's king or one's god made sense because of the severe punishment or remarkable blessing the leader could impart.

In contrast, *Character-Based Leaders* successfully influence others regardless of, sometimes even in spite of, their positions. The strength of the Character-Based Leader is found in the vision they cast and the means they use to bring that vision to life. For Character-Based Leaders, how we get there is as important as where we are going. Commanding others to come can be counterproductive. Instead, the Character-Based Leader seeks to bring people along.

The positional leader views power or authority as a finite resource to be gained, guarded and *never* given away. Character-Based Leaders recognize the truth: Influence isn't measured by the positions we achieve, but by the people we empower to accomplish the vision.

Acting in a humble manner is not the same as being humiliated. This is the first misconception about humility that a leader must overcome. Ancient cultures rarely speak of the kind of humility we admire today. In these honor-bound societies, lowering oneself before a peer or subordinate was an affront to the station and status that the individual, family or nation had fought to obtain. Humility was seen as a surrender of power rather than as a source of it. That's the misconception.

Although we may bleed less, our modern struggle to advance our own careers or influence is no less hard fought than the battles of the ancients. Humility is counterintuitive because it seems to be the relinquishing of power rather than the advancement of it.

As we move forward in history, we see our view of humility transformed. The self-evident truths of the inherent value and unalienable rights of all people have reshaped our governments and our culture. With people free to govern themselves, leadership is redefined. What the king used to win by might, must now be won through influence. Humility is turned on its head. Emptying oneself for the benefit of another becomes an effective means of exponentially increasing one's influence with others.

> *Acting in a humble manner is not the same as being humiliated.*

It also becomes elusive. This is the second misconception. With this new dynamic, humility can be as self-serving as it is virtuous. It seems the more one tries to achieve humility, the more removed from true humility one becomes. This view makes humility the impossible dream, the unachievable goal. Humility is diminished. It is corrupted and misrepresented as a passive-aggressive attempt to increase influence. I've heard it said that true humility isn't thinking highly or lowly of yourself. True humility isn't thinking of yourself at all. As poetic and sentimental as that statement may be, it's also naïve. Rick Warren in his book, *The Purpose Driven Life* begins, "It's not about you." It's true; it's *not* about you. Everything about your life involves you intimately and directly, however. At some level, your ability to function out of humility and to serve another connects with a willful and deliberate decision on your part. Choosing to act in a humble manner does not diminish the virtue of the act. On the contrary, the depth of our humility is ultimately defined by the choices we make.

The world admires Mother Teresa as a modern example of humility. Her work with the poor of Calcutta is legendary. Her advocacy for the rights of the under-resourced has reshaped how the world thinks about meeting the needs of others. Her humble work has had worldwide effect, and this effect was a matter of choice. She chose to take the vows that would make her a nun. She chose to see the need all around her. At great personal cost to herself, she chose to do the thing no one else would do in order to accomplish the mission no one else would take. It was a choice. It was an active pursuit of humility.

This leads to my preferred definition of humility, according to John Dickson: "Humility is the noble choice to forgo your status, deploy your resources or use your influence for the good of others before yourself." In other words, humility is the willing choice to hold power in service of others.

Practical Steps to Grow in Humility

Once we agree that humility is an active choice and that making that choice doesn't somehow reduce our power or corrupt the virtue of that choice, we begin to understand that humility is something that can be practiced and pursued.

Within world religions, Christianity looks to a Jewish carpenter as a remarkable example of choosing humility. The Christian faith maintains that this carpenter was more than a man. He was God in the flesh. As the story goes, he makes a series of choices, each choice more humble than the next.

1. He chooses to set aside his authority and power as God to become a man.
2. He chooses to set aside his rights as a man to become a servant, a slave to others.
3. He chooses, in spite of his innocence, to take another's place for crimes he didn't commit and to suffer a criminal's death by the cruelest form of capital punishment that history has ever produced.

This same carpenter taught that we should love our neighbors and our enemies. He told his followers that the greatest among them would be the servant of all. It wasn't his teaching that captured the imagination of the world, however. It was his example. With each choice, he set aside something of deep personal value: his authority, his rights, his integrity. Yet, in giving these things away, he fulfilled the very purpose of his mission. In humility, he gave away without giving up and still got exactly what he wanted. From his example, we find practical wisdom for growing in humility.

Know Yourself

For humility to be anything more than humiliation, you must begin with an honest assessment of your own authority, ability, capacity and resources. It starts with the question "What do I have to give?" It's impossible to make the noble choice to hold power for the benefit of others if you don't know the power you hold. Don't limit this evaluation to your authority, position or station. Examine your abilities, resources and capacity. What's your potential? What skills do you have? Who you are, what you know, and the things you have can be deployed for the benefit of others. Know yourself.

See the Need

In both of the examples I've cited, the subjects, Mother Teresa and Jesus, saw the need around them. They didn't view people as obstacles to overcome, objects to manipulate, or commodities to trade. They looked into the crowd and were moved with compassion. They saw the need and realized they had within them the capacity to meet that need.

Let's pause here for a moment. Seeing the need is not as easy as we might think. Our perception of the need is influenced by our worldview. Author and feminist leader Anais Nin said, "We don't see things as they are, we see them as we are." We stumble into false humility when we apply our power to imaginary needs that accomplish our own agendas rather than providing solutions for those we try to serve.

If what we have is money, our solution to every problem may involve writing a check. If what we know is technology, our solution will likely involve another gadget. Medical studies have noted that, when specialists diagnose an unknown medical condition in the same patient, cardiologists are more likely to find cardiovascular problems while neurologists are more likely to find neurological causes. Sometimes the real problem is masked by the way we view it. The humble choice may lead us to learn a new skill or to collaborate with someone who has different resources or a different worldview. Whatever the case, for us to hold power for the benefit of others, that power must be appropriately applied to the appropriate need. Can you identify the needs in your corporation or community? Which obstacles discourage or distract your coworkers? What solution, regardless of reward, could you provide for a client today? Find the need and do something about it.

Dignify Indignity

Several years ago, as CEO of the Walt Disney Corporation, Michael Eisner instituted a policy regarding the Disney parks: Keeping the parks sparkling clean was a high priority. Any Disney cast member seen walking past and ignoring a piece of trash on the ground could be immediately fired. As a guest of the *TODAY Show*, Eisner stood with Matt Lauer on Main Street in the heart of the Magic Kingdom. During the live interview and surrounded by park guests, Eisner spotted a piece of trash on the ground, politely excused himself, picked up the trash, and deposited it in the nearest trash can.

For a brief moment, Eisner became the highest paid custodian in the Disney Corporation. Certainly, his choice was in line with the Disney policy he had initiated, but consider the moment. He was in the middle of a live, nationwide television interview. Consider his position. He was the CEO. The dignity of his position and the timing of the circumstance gave him every reason to ignore the trash on the ground and to expect someone else to handle it, but he didn't. He made the humble choice to dignify indignity. He served his company and park guests while providing an example for everyone to see.

For us to grow in humility, we must sometimes make undignified choices. This lack of dignity doesn't come from a disrespect of position or denial of authority, but from a willingness to do what needs to be done regardless of responsibility. An ancient proverb says, "Where there are no oxen, the stall is clean, but strength comes by many oxen." Being willing to graciously shovel through the glorious mess that is humanity makes room for strength and magnifies the dignity of our positions. Are there jobs you refuse to do because they belong to someone else? Will you get dirty to meet the needs of others? In what ways can you lower yourself to add value to those around you? To hold power for the benefit of others, we must dignify indignity.

Make the Choice

In a letter to the church in Philippi, a missionary once wrote, "Let nothing be done through selfish ambition or vain conceit. Rather, in humility value others above yourself. Let each of you look out not only for his own interests, but also for the interests of others." What you *can* do speaks to your ability; what you *should* do, to your moral responsibility. What you *choose* to do is a reflection of your character.

This is the essence of humility: to make the noble choice to forgo your status, deploy your resources, or use your influence for the good of others before the good of yourself. It is a quality of character that can be practiced and pursued. You can lead without humility, but you cannot be a Character-Based Leader without it. Humility is a worthy choice to make.

Chapter 15

Respect: Bring Your Team to Life

Mike Henry Sr.

What Is Respect?

Wikipedia defines respect as "both a positive feeling of esteem for a person or other entity... and also specific actions and conduct representative of that esteem." Respect is hoping the other person wins.

Respect is the pursuit of a win-win outcome. When we respect others, we hold positive feelings of esteem for them, and that feeling causes us to act in their best interests until that interest causes real harm to us. My respect for my coworkers enables me to seek win-win-win outcomes in every relationship. By win-win-win, I mean each individual wins and the organization wins too. In fact,

> *Respect is the proper outcome of humility. It recognizes individuality and can always be given because the supply is endless.*

I sometimes use an image of WIN^n, where n equals the number of stakeholders in any effort. Sustainable, Character-Based Leadership doesn't want to win at the expense of others. We look for ways where everyone can win.

If everyone is looking for ways for everyone to win, a lot of positive energy results. When you're a Character-Based Leader, you bring respect. As a result, you often get much more of it in return too.

Respect is something I can always give away. The supply is endless, unless I end it. Character-Based Leaders produce leadership qualities from who they are rather than from their positions or power. Position and power are scarce, but character, although rare, is abundant. Nothing is reduced when we produce more quality character. We bring energy, even life, to our world when we take the best of who we are and give it away. Respect is not a natural quality. Left to ourselves, we tend to draw two inaccurate conclusions about others and ourselves: We believe either that we're the center of the universe (or very near the center) or that we're not even in it. When we think we're at the center of the universe, we err on the side of over-importance, and when we think we're unimportant, we miss on the low side. Both errors are dangerous.

Respect is the proper outcome of humility. Too much humility, and we under-appreciate ourselves and over-respect others. Too little humility, and we under-appreciate others and over-respect ourselves. *Humility* comes from an accurate understanding of where we fit in the universe, and *respect* is what we give others when we accurately understand where they fit.

Respect recognizes individuality. Individually, we are, in some degree, able to control our destinies while we are at the same time dependent on others and on circumstances outside our control. We are free to choose, but we always bring more energy when we freely choose. Respect motivates because everyone gives more and better effort than they would ever let a boss or an organization demand.

In the end, the best benefit of respect is that it fuels trust. Trust lubricates relationships. Trusting relationships are resilient. They can withstand difficulty. Trust eliminates the friction between people, enabling them to work as a team.

Common Respect Mistakes

Like most Character-Based Leadership attributes, respect is something we do because of who we are. The most common mistakes regarding respect occur when we attempt to manufacture respect, either for others or for ourselves.

Manufacturing Respect for Others

If we try to act as if we respect someone by producing the specific actions and conduct representative of respect, we instantly become hypocrites. We may reap some benefit from the president of our company thinking that we respect him or her, but inside, we kill a little of our true selves every day. Hypocrisy kills you on the inside. Your actions sap your very energy, and the thing you do to gain actually costs you more than it produces.

Practicing Comparison

When we practice comparison, we fall into a subtle trap. If we only respect those who "measure up" or who compare favorably to ourselves, we really don't respect anyone. We remain at the center of every evaluation. We only respect our judgments of those other people, expecting others to respect us in the same way. However, since we're still in the center of the valuation, we are faking the respect. That type of "I respect you because you're better than me" respect is selfish and fails to generate any energy.

Demanding Respect

Another error is demanding respect outright. Focus on yourself, and that's all you will have. Focus on others, and you gain them and yourself. When someone demands respect, I am tempted to withhold it instantly. Once, while managing a warehouse, I noticed a temporary worker doing a sloppy job. I asked him what he was doing, and he told me he was doing his job the way he wanted to. Not wanting to invest a lot of time and energy in this person, I suggested that he needed to call it a day and ask his temporary service to put him somewhere else tomorrow because we wouldn't need his services any longer today or in the future.

"What?" he asked.

"You can leave," I answered.

"You can't talk to me like that. You need to talk to me with respect. I don't have to take that from you," he responded.

"Alright, you can leave, sir," I replied.

The rest of the exchange probably shouldn't be reprinted.

No one wants to have respect demanded, manipulated, coerced or cajoled out of them. It's just not proper. Respect is like a butterfly. You can chase it. You can try to tell it where to go and what to do, but in the end, it will show up when you stop looking for it and pursuing it. Respect others and do things worthy of respect, and then respect will appear.

Applying Respect

Everyone is free to choose how much they contribute. No one, even your direct reports or your children, follows your every direction or every wish. They choose to follow, serve, help or obey. The older your children get, the more they choose. Much is written about strong-willed children, those who choose to go their own ways sometimes to their own detriment. Certainly, children should understand that their parents only wish them well, yet how many of us rebelled in ways that created harm? Teenagers are simply adult-interns. They get to practice being an adult while (hopefully) their parents manage their choices and mitigate the consequences of their actions. Regardless, we are all free to choose how much we cooperate with others.

Don't Choose Who; Choose How Much

We are also free to choose how much we respect others. When we look down our noses or judge others, our inward focus drains energy from others. Others will contribute energy into an effort that energizes the group. After a while, if they contribute energy into an effort that only benefits a few, people begin to resist or to hold back their best efforts. Other people are unique entities. They're free (regardless of circumstances) to choose their attitudes and actions. Their pasts, presents, resources, circumstances and experiences may limit them, but that never makes them *less than* I am. When we respect others, we choose to have positive feelings of esteem for them. Giving genuine esteem brings energy and life to the relationship, and our actions follow.

Endless Source

Character-Based Leadership is an endless source of energy and life for an organization. From character comes several unlimited resources, respect being one. We genuinely respect others by finding something for which we can truly have a generous, positive feeling of esteem toward them. If the feeling is genuine and if we have any integrity (consistently acting according to our beliefs), then we create specific actions and conduct representative of that esteem. We will act with respect toward those we respect. We will create actions that demonstrate respect and bring energy and life to our organization.

If we fail to respect others, we cut off that energy source. When all of our focus and efforts are on ourselves, individually, we become empty shells draining energy from our organizations or families. If the drain continues unchecked, it will kill all of the life around us.

When large numbers of people fail to respect others, the infrastructure and even the community deteriorates. No doubt you've seen the blight of some cities. You know what I'm talking about; it's where the buildings are empty and the windows are broken. There is no life and no interest. That blight occurs when people take more than they give. Over time, they drain the life out of a neighborhood. Companies end up like that too. Companies that take more than they give become empty places that sap the life out of everyone who works there, and every relationship becomes transactional.

Focus only on yourself, and you'll lose the ability to bring energy and life to your relationships. Practice respect and bring life.

Respect in Action: Conflict

Conflict is inevitable. I've come to realize that we all have different ways of dealing with conflict. We seem to deal with conflict in ways that developed while we were young, in our families of origin. The styles vary based on the nature of the conflict and on our relationships with the

115

other parties involved. We developed these default methods growing up and generally favor our default method throughout our lives unless we mature enough to adopt new and more effective methods.

Also, depending on our experience and maturity, we develop opinions about how others deal with conflict. People who use different methods of dealing with conflict seem, at least to us, to be going about it the wrong way until we see them experience success. Depending on your level of arrogance, you may think that others all deal with conflict better or worse than you do. Unless they partake of conflict the same way you do, you'll always think they're wrong at least in some degree.

There are many ways of dealing with conflict. We even apply different methods with different people. We deal with our spouses one way, with our parents another, and with our kids yet another. We deal with vendors one way, with peers at work another, with subordinates a third way, and with authority figures still another way. Although we can judge behaviors based on results, we need to consider both the other people and the results of our interactions to find the best ways of handling conflict. Bad ways of handling conflict manipulate others and therefore fail to create a sustainable result. Any method that fails to create a win-win outcome is less than desirable. The method, however, isn't always the reason for bad results. Some people won't allow win-win, but those people don't validate or invalidate methods. Assuming you have reasonable coworkers in healthy relationships pursuing worthwhile goals, win-win outcomes are always possible.

Some bad methods of dealing with conflict include avoidance, bullying and coercion, the ABC's of bad conflict management. Remember, our goal isn't to manipulate or to simply win, but to reach a win-win outcome.

Rather than focus on style, I'd like to compare the Character-Based Leader's approach and the positional leader's approach to dealing with conflict, specifically with relationships in an organizational (work) context.

Start with Respect

Character-Based Leaders earn their influence from who they are, not their position in the organization. Therefore, a Character-Based Leader wants to avoid using position as a lever or a tool to manipulate. When conflict arises, focus on restoring peace. I don't mean peace as an absence of discord, but rather as the peace of a level playing field or a mutual understanding. In other words, demonstrate respect first. Separate the disagreement from the individuals involved. They're still people. They have the same right to space, time and energy in the workplace as you do. They're your equal. Avoid the urge to defend or maintain your position, and respect the other person enough to understand his or her point of view in the disagreement. You may not disagree as much as you think.

Employ that well-known habit #5 of the *Seven Habits of Highly Effective People* by Steven R. Covey, "Seek first to understand, then to be understood." By showing respect for the other person and his or her reasoning, you give yourself the best chance to learn. One way to eliminate conflict is to change *your mind* and agree. By respecting the other person's opinion and listening to the full story, you can restore peace by agreeing.

In contrast, positional leaders begin with the idea that their perspective gains credibility and believability based on their position; therefore, the higher the position, the better the idea. Companies the size of Enron and WorldCom fell for this reason; no one challenged the individuals in the positions of authority, so their ideas were followed based on pragmatism rather than based on values or beliefs. People got swept up in the top-down, positional authority, and it happens every day.

I used to work in an industry where it was commonly understood that individuals might have to break the law to satisfy the customer. Everyone did what was expected, but no leader was accountable for the understanding or behavior of the people doing the actual work.

Present New Information

By understanding others first, a Character-Based Leader can focus, with respect, on why a disagreement remains. Maybe that disagreement is a result of some knowledge you just learned and you need to acknowledge your lack of understanding and reach an agreement, or maybe you place a different value or forecast a different result than the other person does.

If you have some understanding that isn't shared by the other person, present that information gracefully. You should be in a better position to be understood because you just gave that grace to the other person or group involved. Maybe you need to introduce some new information, or maybe you simply have a different opinion about the information than the other person does. Work to fill any gaps in knowledge, understanding or assumptions.

One way to avoid escalating the conflict is to ask genuine questions. The difference between a genuine question and a confrontational question is first in its purpose. If your question is designed to expose the other's ignorance or some other manipulation, you come across like a lawyer and you incite a defensive response. But if you can genuinely seek to further your understanding about what the other person understands, you can reduce tension and move toward agreement.

Consider two questions: "Did you consider factor X?" and "What do you think about factor X, since you didn't mention it?" The second is clearly more along the lines of seeking understanding. Diffusing confrontation gives you the invitation to introduce Factor X if it hadn't been considered. "Why, no... Do you think Factor X is an issue?" might be a response that opens the door to ending the conflict. Other questions that arise from a genuine desire to know will help close the gaps. "Do you think such-and-such isn't a risk?" Have the same attitude you just modeled, and continue to treat the other person as an equal in the conversation. If they change their mind with the new information, you've resolved the issue and maintained, maybe even improved, the relationship.

Positional leaders seldom ask questions, believing that if they admit they don't know something, that's a sign of weakness. Positional leaders wear masks so they "look the part" and therefore can't learn anything new. For a positional leader to stay in his or her position, the leader must remind everyone else of that position. This is especially dangerous when junior members of the team become aware of new information. Limited in their ability to present the information or to influence decisions made "above" them, they eventually become passive, assuming that their leadership has no interest, or, in the best case, they leave and find someplace where some information and influence can flow up the organizational chart.

Disagree with Respect

In the end, you may still disagree with the other person. You've both got jobs to do, and depending on the relationship and the final decision that is reached, you and your coworker may need to agree to disagree, manage the disagreement, and execute the plan. Try to remain open to learning. You must be at least willing to learn and hear if you want to teach and be heard. Your willingness to remain open to new inputs provides the best assurance that the other person will remain open to new information too. Either way, there are three scenarios that call for different methods of dealing with conflict in this state. Each method is related to the conflict, your relationship with the other person, and the conflict's ability to obstruct the objectives of the organization.

Scenario 1: Incidental Conflict

First, is the conflict an obstacle to achieving the organization's objectives, or does it violate a core value? If not and if you and your coworker can achieve team objectives without resolving the conflict, then do so. Achieve the objectives with excellence and revisit your disagreement another day. Success minimizes conflict, so even if you disagree and achieve your objectives, you can be a strong team.

Scenario 2: Peer-Level Disagreement

If the disagreement is critical to reaching objectives, you have another consideration. Is your conflict with a peer, with a subordinate, or with someone higher up in the organization? (Yes, position still plays a role.) If you and the person with whom you disagree are peers, try to agree on a method of arbitration or escalation. This continues the respect you've started to build. If possible, maybe even submit to the method of arbitration that the other person suggests. If the arbitrator agrees with your plan, there will be no further argument. Escalate with respect.

Scenario 3: Subordinate Disagreement

Finally, if the disagreement is critical and you and the other person are at different levels (manager vs. director, for example), there is still one additional consideration for the Character-Based Leader. Regardless of your position, give the other person the benefit of the doubt and proceed with respect. If you are senior (a director, for example), encourage the other person to involve his or her director. You want to reach the best objective, correct? If you escalate to the other person's director, you risk making the manager look bad. (There are potential variances here based on who you know and what types of relationships you have.) You might also get an impartial VP or other senior leader involved to present a third opinion. In every case, be as transparent as possible and seek the best decision for the organization. The more respect you show and the less you demand, the greater chance that you will come through the conflict with strong relationships that are able to achieve future objectives.

If you're the junior member of the conflict, continue the conflict carefully. It may be that you just need to do what you've been told and to act as if the conflict isn't a critical obstacle. Let's face it: If you can choose to do what you've been told, you might give that some serious consideration and achieve the objectives. Don't passively resist doing what you're told and allow failure. Make the organization successful. After you've contributed significantly to the overall success, you may actually get another opportunity to revisit the original conflict and to show the value of your initial recommendations. Your primary objective is to find a way to make your organization and the other senior person in the conflict successful.

If (as the junior member of the conflict) you're still convinced that the objective is in jeopardy, ask the senior person in the conflict to help you make sure this is a success. You can ask if the senior member would please allow you to engage one of their peers or an impartial senior executive for a second opinion. Asking is the key, as this respects the senior person's position and authority in the organization. Only when you're sure failure is certain can you consider any nuclear option such as going around or over this senior person. Exercise every effort to follow the rule mentioned above about transparency.

Positional Leaders and Conflict

Positional leaders see conflict as an assault on their position. Their initial reactions are almost always defensive. A positional leader must get the point across to you that disagreeing is a bad career move. Positional leaders cannot let you move up until you learn the importance of the people in those "up" positions in the first place. To positional leaders, conflict is a signal that they must restore "order" and get everyone back into their boxes on the organizational chart.

Respect is the key to bringing life to a team and to giving everyone in the organization an opportunity to lead in some sphere. If we claim we need more leaders, but fail to give people room to lead, we're fooling ourselves. You can make leaders out of your team and your peers by demonstrating respect and growing through conflict. Respect your team members, and your leadership will grow through the additional input, insight and perspective. Respect others, and create teams where members flourish. Conflict, like exercise, builds muscle rather than scar tissue, and your team and your leadership will grow as a result.

Chapter 16

Leadership Touchstones

Jennifer V. Miller

In ancient times, people who wanted to determine the value of a metal such as gold would use a touchstone to determine the purity of the metal. To perform the test, they would scrape the metal

> *"Trust is the lubrication that makes it possible for organizations to work."*
> ~Warren Bennis

against a dark stone and look at the marks that the metal left. They would then compare the marks on the touchstone to an existing sample of gold to decide if the gold met their criteria for quality.

In much the same way, people in organizations have interpersonal benchmarks they use to evaluate the trustworthiness of their leaders. It's like a touchstone for trust. As Warren Bennis said, "Trust is the lubrication that makes it possible for organizations to work." Leaders who don't measure up are deemed lacking in that "social lubricant."

Scholars and management consultants like Bennis, Jim Kouzes, Barry Posner, and many others have been talking about the long, slow decline of employee trust in leadership for the past 15 years, according to the DDI World White Paper "Trust in the Workplace" from 2003. Severe economic downturns in 2008 caused by bad financial decisions have made a precarious situation even worse. In 2011, Maritz Research, a leader in employee-satisfaction research, reported in one of their white papers (the Maritz Research Hospitality Group Employee Engagement Poll, 2011) that 25% of employees had less trust in their management than in 2010. (And in 2010, they were also reporting less trust than in earlier years, so the trend is moving in the wrong direction!)

Clearly, leaders face an uphill battle in winning back employees' trust. So, as a leader, how do you know if you make the trustworthiness grade?

Just as people used different types of stones years ago to assess the quality of metal, employees today use a variety of touchstones to determine a leader's trustworthiness. Metaphorically speaking, each person is toting around a handful of stones that help them decide whether to trust their leaders. When people interact with you, they are rubbing those stones against your leadership actions to determine the quality of your trustworthiness. I call these internal barometers *Trust Touchstones™*. If you want to be a truly influential leader, it pays to know what these stones are.

Strictly speaking, Trust Touchstones are as unique as the individuals using them, but leaders can still use the three touchstones that follow to help assess whether their actions are building trusting relationships with people in their organization.

Trust Touchstones fall into one of three broad categories:

- Ethics
- Interpersonal
- Work Focus

Ethics Touchstone

The *Ethics Touchstone* evaluates a leader's moral compass: Does he follow an appropriate ethical code? Does she seem honest? Does this leader treat people with respect, act with accountability, and avoid blaming others? If so, people will consider this leader trustworthy after applying the ethics-based trust touchstone.

At this point, you're most likely thinking, *Well, I've got this touchstone covered. I'm a completely ethical person. Let's move on to the next touchstone.*

Not so fast! Let's examine this thought a bit more closely. Have you ever encountered a leader who genuinely thought that he was *un*ethical?

Probably not. Now, please understand, I'm not suggesting that you are unethical, but isn't it possible that your moral compass has pointed you north when your team member's is pointing northeast?

Take, for example, the case of Kathy and Chad. They are colleagues who work for the same company, but in different departments. Kathy is the project leader for a cross-functional team that's in charge of implementing a new system-wide software upgrade. Chad is on the team as a technical advisor. During one meeting in which the team is discussing the workload of several outside contractors, Kathy says, "Hey, I'm not really worried about burning them out. That's why we hire subcontractors—to get extra hands. If the workload is too much, they should have thought of that before they gave us the quote." Chad rubs his Ethics Touchstone up against this comment and thinks, *That's not right. I think we should pay all people—internal employees and external contractors—fairly. Kathy seems really mercenary. I'd better be sure I'm careful when I quote any future projects with her.*

From Kathy's perspective, she's protecting the interests of her company and keeping her project on budget. That's certainly a valid goal, and well within what she sees as her moral standards. Chad sees it differently, though. Kathy's stance on contractors—"They should have thought of that before they gave us the quote"—violates his sense of fair business standards. Therefore, he's feeling distrustful of future interactions with her.

Most people in the work world are pretty clear about the "biggies" in ethics: you don't steal, you don't lie, and you treat people decently. This scenario represents those ethical shades of gray that can create tension between leaders and their followers.

A leader's ethics are one of the foundational ingredients of Character-Based Leadership. If a leader doesn't demonstrate ethical behavior every day, then it would be difficult to call him or her a Character-Based Leader. It's like making a chocolate chip cookie recipe without the chocolate chips. Sure, the end result is a cookie, but it's not a *chocolate chip* cookie.

The Ethics Touchstone is the most commonly applied touchstone. Indeed, a person's moral compass is a very important factor in determining whether we trust them or not, but it's not the only measuring stick people are using, and that's where some leaders come up short in building trust with their teams and colleagues. Think of the Ethics Touchstone as containing the basic ingredients of healthy working relationships. Following the recipe analogy, the next two touchstones are the "secret sauce" that gives a leader that extra special something in the trust-building recipe.

Interpersonal Touchstone

The second type of trust touchstone, the *Interpersonal Touchstone*, comes from the interpersonal chemistry that people feel when interacting with their leaders. It's based largely on a leader's interpersonal style: that blend of individual personality traits and daily interactions that comprise the way he or she connects with others in the organization.

No doubt, we've all interacted with leaders with whom we just didn't click. You might call it a personality conflict. Sometimes we just don't take to certain people. How does this play into the way people gauge their trust levels with leaders? Here are two examples.

Some leaders are naturally extroverted. They are gregarious and enthusiastic, making friends easily. To the more introverted person, this outgoing behavior may potentially come off as fake, leading the person to conclude that the leader is not genuine and is therefore untrustworthy.

An introverted leader may seem standoffish, sheltering his or her thoughts. In this case, when interacting with a highly extroverted employee, the leader may seem as if he or she is hiding something, causing the employee to sense that something is being hidden.

A person's personality is at the core of his being, so it's not realistic to expect leaders to try to change their personalities; however, it *is* important for leaders to be aware of how their actions may come across to their team. In the case of a more extroverted leader, he can be aware of overemphasizing enthusiasm, for example, and work to dial it down a bit. In the case of a more reserved leader, she can look for signs that people are skeptical and can be ready to share a bit more information or emotion when needed.

Work Focus Touchstone

The third touchstone, the *Work Focus Touchstone*, is based on what a leader focuses on to get things done at work. This trust touchstone is probably the least understood, and that's a shame because it represents the largest opportunity for building trust with people. That's because leaders can tweak their work focus to fit a specific situation, while their ethics and personality remain fairly constant.

A leader's work focus is based on *behaviors,* and those can be modified to fit the needs of differing team members. Think of it this way: Behaviors are the outward expression of one's interior life. Your leadership behaviors are driven by your values, life experiences, and personality. All of these things shape who you are and inform what you do. It's the "do" part of that statement that your team members are evaluating daily with the work focus touchstone.

I'll illustrate with an example. Let's say that as a leader you highly value collaboration as a way to get things done at work. You believe that creating strong personal relationships is the foundation upon which all other activities must be built; therefore, you invest time in getting to know your employees, both personally and professionally. When you conduct one-on-one meetings, you spend a few minutes inquiring about your employees' hobbies or recent accomplishments outside the workplace. It could be said that your natural inclination is to connect with people in a genuine way, so the focus of how you get things done is the relationship you have with people.

For the sake of continuing this example, let's assume you have a person named Parker who reports to you. Parker has a different work focus, one that is targeted on getting results and forward motion. To Parker, those one-on-one meetings are a bit annoying, because you invest too much time in what he would call chitchat. Parker's touchstone is more focused on the task at hand.

If someone asked Parker if you were trustworthy, the reply using the Ethics Touchstone most likely would be "Of course!" But if the question were "Parker, do you trust your team leader to deliver results in a timely manner?" the reply might be, "Sometimes I think my team leader spends too much time socializing. We have tons of work to do, and I wish we could just get on with it." As you can see, both of you have a work focus touchstone, but it's calibrated differently.

The example above highlights the two broad themes of the Work Focus Touchstone: an emphasis on *task* and an emphasis on *people*. No doubt, you've probably seen this categorization before in some sort of personality profiling or leadership seminar. It's based on research in social psychology of leadership structures that shows that humans tend to have a natural preference that gravitates toward either a focus on "getting things done" (task) or on "interacting with and relating to others" (people). Neither focus is the "correct" one; both are valid viewpoints. The implication for trust-building is that when we encounter people with a different focus than our own, we may tend to ascribe negative intentions to their behavior.

> *Successful leaders can take trust-building to a new level when they pay attention to the unique ways their employees perceive their leader's trustworthiness.*

In the example above, we can see that while there is trust between Parker and the work team leader, there is also a bit of friction. Parker has trust in the work team leader's *ethics*, but doesn't necessarily trust that the work team leader has the right *work focus*.

Effective leaders will take the time to observe and understand their team members' individual work focuses. They will work to help all team members understand that although a focus on task or people is perfectly acceptable as a natural preference, there will be times when the emphasis must be more slanted toward one or the other. A truly skilled leader will also help team members appreciate differing work focuses by encouraging team members of opposite approaches to collaborate and to look to one another as sounding boards.

Here's a story about how using the Work Focus Touchstone plays out in the real world. Bob is a veteran leader who directs the quality efforts for his company's manufacturing plants across the globe. Over the years, Bob has attended training sessions and seminars that focus on personal and professional development. Along the way, he's learned that people have different approaches, outlooks and strengths. Whenever Bob has to assemble a project team, he looks at both the technical capabilities of the potential group members *and* their interpersonal strengths. He's told me that he specifically coaches project team members to seek out someone who "looks at [the issue] from a completely different set of glasses." This is Bob's way of ensuring that both work focuses are represented and seen as valid viewpoints.

Leaders can leverage this underused, but powerful trust-building mechanism to help them interact most effectively with their team, peers, colleagues and customers.

Trust Touchstones: The Bedrock of Character-Based Leadership

When it comes to trustworthiness, it goes without saying that a leader's morals and ethics must be impeccable. That's the bedrock of Character-Based Leadership. Successful leaders can take trust-building to a new level when they pay attention to the unique ways their employees perceive their leader's trustworthiness. By building awareness and leveraging the additional Trust Touchstones of Interpersonal and Work Focus, leaders avoid a one-size-fits-all approach to trust-building with their team members.

Chapter 17

Daily Actions That Cultivate Trust and Collaboration

Sonia DiMaulo

Mistrust versus Trust

Is mistrust today's default position? How easily do we trust others? What words and actions lead us to trust? It's time for a quick self-assessment.

When you meet someone new, do you:

- interpret their words and actions before assessing their character? You give them a chance.
- assume they want something and turn your trust dial to mistrust? This keeps you safe.

> *"The moment there is suspicion about a person's motives, everything he does becomes tainted."*
> *~ Mahatma Gandhi*

- assume they are trustworthy until proven otherwise? You trust them automatically.

When someone new meets you, do you want them to:

- interpret your words and actions before assessing your character?
- assume you want something and turn their trust dial to mistrust?
- assume you are trustworthy until proven otherwise?

What would happen if we trust first, connect first, give first? Only good things happen in this environment. I know this because it is one of my most important guiding principles. This character-based principle helps me to make better and stronger connections with everyone I meet, from a colleague to a bank teller. People respond positively toward people who trust first, which makes my world a happier place to live, work, and play.

If I am unique and mistrust is today's default position, then gaining someone's trust is a privilege. Trust from others develops over time once you can prove that your actions match your words. Consistent actions and follow-up on those actions are the true measures of trust.

What Is Trust?

Defining trust is difficult. Understanding what trust is through demonstrating or observing specific actions helps us better understand its significance and recognize its value. "It is a feeling of certainty that a person or thing will not fail. *Trust* implies depth and assurance of feeling that is often based on inconclusive evidence." (The Free Dictionary by Farlex) The explanation is enhanced further: Trust is the firm reliance on and confidence in the integrity, ability, character, worth, or reliability of a person or thing.

To provide my perspective of the definition of trust and why it's needed, I will share two stories that are based on experiences in my career.

Jeff was new on the job. After ten years with the same company, he was embarking on a new adventure. He was excited but apprehensive, which is normal for work in a new environment. He was concerned about how he would fit in, what his colleagues were really like, and how he would lead his team to greatness. Within his first weeks on the job, he was scheduled to attend an industry conference. While he recognized some familiar faces, he didn't know anyone really well. He decided to keep it cool and confident and to take on the role of observer.

While Jeff was speaking with a vendor during the trade show, a familiar face approached. The man, who was a senior vice president at Jeff's new company, started speaking with the vendor about Jeff. Jeff stared in disbelief as he listened. The man began listing Jeff's strengths. Jeff thought, *How does he know this about me?*

Jeff entered a period of deep reflection as he walked away from the conversation. Here are his thoughts:

- I didn't realize I was perceived in this way.
- He only focused on my strengths.
- I need to live up to his expectations!
- I didn't realize people were observing me so closely.
- How does this SVP know so much? The communication flow at this company is unique!
- I like how this company operates.
- Starting this new job is turning out to be the best decision I have ever made.
- I now feel empowered to lead my team.
- I need to be strategic and thoughtful about how my actions and words are perceived.
- I need to create a strategy for providing and receiving feedback continually so I can empower my employees in the same way.

Jeff is self-aware, engaged and planning for success. A one-minute conversation did all that! He is now in the right zone for human flourishing. According to Dr. Barbara Fredrickson from the University of North Carolina at Chapel Hill, "Human Flourishing is to live within an optimal range of human functioning, one that connotes goodness... growth and resilience." A low-stress environment allows people to use their whole brain (emotion and reason) for more creative and ethical decisions.

Let's dissect the encounter further. The SVP has cultivated trust and collaboration in Jeff.

- Jeff can now more easily trust the SVP and, by association, the company.
- His willingness to collaborate with members of his team has been given a boost.
- His respect for the SVP has increased.
- He is now able to focus on his own strengths as perceived by others.
- He has been given a model by which to lead his own team.
- His ability to make ethical and sound decisions is also enhanced.

Why Trust?

> *In its basic form, the purpose of an organization is to work together to accomplish that which one cannot do alone. Feedback is an essential process to the organization's success. In cybernetics, feedback that promotes change is positive feedback. Negative feedback is intended to maintain the status quo and limit change.* ~ **Donella Meadows**, **Thinking in Systems - A Primer**

If Donella Meadows is correct, then cultivating trust and collaboration and establishing feedback processes that promote change through positive feedback should be at the top of every organization's agenda. Providing authentic feedback that gets used and ultimately affects organizations, work and worker performance can be an excellent way to cultivate trust and collaboration.

The Dark Side

What would happen if your daily actions were scrutinized and criticized with the aim to elevate awareness of your performance gaps and to enhance your performance?

Let's look at Carole's story.

Carole ran a very high-profile meeting with members of her global team. Carole had worked very hard on preparing for the meeting's success. Given the prominence of this meeting, a few members of the senior management team were also present. At the end of the first day of meetings, they had a quick feedback session to assess wins and to present improvements for Day 2.

The feedback instantly started with things Carole should have done and things she had not done well. Although she knew the day had not been perfect, she was not expecting a barrage of negative comments. Her face visibly showed her disappointment. As the comments continued, her energy faded and wilted.

How was she feeling now about delivering Day 2 of the meeting? She may have been feeling discouraged and depressed, and certainly not looking forward to the feedback session on Day 2!

Then Adam, her peer, decided to help boost her morale. He shared with her a few things he thought she had done rather well (focused on strengths) and then delivered one item that she could try improving on Day 2: voice projection. The next morning, Carole focused solely on voice projection and noticed a considerable difference in her confidence and in the participants' engagement. At lunch, she approached Adam to ask him about her voice projection and then, encouraged and excited, she asked him for another improvement tip to try that afternoon.

The dark side of feedback has extremely detrimental effects, including the breach of trust. If we hear only negative remarks, human flourishing wilts and dies. We may feel that others do not trust us, and then we may start to question our trust in others. In this environment, Carole's performance cannot affect business goals. In fact, her performance will take a nosedive before it can thrive again, if at all, and her commitment to the organization and to leadership will also falter.

What is the cost of this disengagement? Tom Rath, author of *StrengthsFinder 2.0* for the *Gallup Management Journal*, provides the following statistics:

- The employee's chances of being actively disengaged are 40% if the manager primarily ignores the employee.
- The employee's chances of being actively disengaged are 22% if the manager primarily focuses on the employee's weaknesses.
- The employee's chances of being actively disengaged are only 1% if the manager focuses on the employee's strengths.

Why trust others? It's simple: Leaders who trust their people's professional integrity and believe that each one works hard make it easier for everyone to see the team as a unit. Properly assigning tasks based on strengths will elevate the engagement of the individuals and of the team to professional excellence. My experience shows that employees who trust their leaders and teammates will perform better and more collaboratively than those who do not have that trust.

Simple to explain, difficult to execute. So what's your plan?

Daily Tips for Cultivating Trust and Collaboration

As a leader or peer, it's important to view your daily actions as food. Toxins will overpower growth and eventually destroy the ability to thrive and flourish. The right amount of authentic care cultivates healthy organisms that can sustain periods of drought. In other words, your daily actions are powerful: they can be the determining factor in developing a highly engaged team that thrives and succeeds.

What are you feeding the people around you? How do they perceive your actions?

Step 1: Thoughtfully select actions that cultivate trust and collaboration. (Start with the list of 25 actions below.)

Step 2: Get feedback!

This list of 25 strategies will help you to influence positive results and to cultivate trust and collaboration in your teams. The list was generated by asking LinkedIn users the following:

Share your best practice: What advice would you provide your colleague, employee, family member or friend who is looking for ways to influence their peers successfully?

Which best practices do you value?

1. Understand their personality type and yours.
2. Be respectful of their values.
3. Listen to verbal/non-verbal feedback.
4. Create a mission statement for your life.
5. Be real when you meet others.
6. Protect your integrity.
7. Let your peers win!
8. Give willingly and fully.
9. Offer something useful.
10. Show empathy.
11. Adopt one goal at a time.
12. Follow through and be consistent.
13. Never unjustly take advantage for the sake of achieving the goal.
14. The best way to build influence is to genuinely care about others. To listen, to understand, and to be helpful to them.
15. Demonstrate grace and integrity.

16. Your actions speak louder than words.
17. Find out what motivates people.
18. Figure out what's in it for them.
19. Allow people to pass you by, to learn, to make mistakes, and to criticize you, and help each other.
20. Empower others.
21. Be the message.
22. Influence those you come into contact with by displaying genuine character.
23. Get to know your peers; ask questions.
24. Identify areas of commonality.
25. Understand your own skills and communication style.

> *Would you like me to give you a formula for success? It's quite simple, really. Double your rate of failure. You are thinking of failure as the enemy of success. But it isn't at all. You can be discouraged by failure or you can learn from it, so go ahead and make mistakes. Make all you can. Because remember that's where you will find success.* ~ **Thomas J. Watson**

Here is my formula for success:

1. Empower others and find ways to help them flourish. Keep trying various strategies and make mistakes until you find the options that work for you and the people around you. Authenticity in your words and actions is the only way trust can develop.

2. Find out how your actions are perceived. Although it's hard at first, asking for feedback and demonstrating that you have considered the feedback is a *powerful* strategy that can help cultivate trusting and collaborative relationships.

> *I learned that trust truly does change everything. Once you create trust, genuine character - and competency-based trust - almost everything else falls into place.* ~ **Stephen M.R. Covey**, **The Speed of Trust: The One Thing That Changes Everything**

A few years ago, I made someone's day by giving her the benefit of the doubt (and assumed that she had a good reason for her decision) in front of her client. She approached me afterward and explained how touched she was that I "believed in her."

Plan to build great relationships; don't just expect them to happen magically.

Chapter 18

The Language of Leadership

Georgia Feiste

*To improve communications, work not on the utterer but
the recipient.*
~ Peter Drucker

We are a nation, perhaps even a civilization, that has embarked on the impersonal, conversational world of e-mail, Facebook, Twitter and LinkedIn. If we are lucky, we will also interact via telephone or Skype, or even face to face. While this has expanded our ability to communicate with others on a worldwide basis, it may have diluted our ability to develop long and lasting relationships with our coworkers and customers.

Why do I say that? Because *it is the person who receives the communication that communicates.* Unless there is someone to *hear*, there is no communication. There is only a posting, written words within an e-mail, or noise. And without communication, there is no relationship.

Although I have not done or read any scientific studies attesting to my convictions, I believe that the failure to communicate is primarily based in a failure to listen. When we listen, we hear information and facts, feelings and often needs. When we concentrate, we hear requests. Since these are aspects of conversation that are critical to understanding, we must be willing to drop our expectations about what we expect to observe and make the conversation genuine and heartfelt.

Susan Scott, author of *Fierce Conversations*, tells us "the conversation is the relationship." The key, then, is not only to listen with your whole being, but also to create an environment that encourages others to listen to you and to each other. This is an environment built on deep and abiding relationships, an environment based on unprecedented trust.

There are five principles of Character-Based Leadership that continually draw my attention because they are at the very heart of a leader's ability to demonstrate the gifts of inspiration, encouragement, and guidance to take a team to success. They all require the art of communication: a conversation that *is* the relationship. This, then, is the language of leadership.

> *The art of communication is the language of leadership.*
> ~ *James Humes*

Balance

The first principle is *balance*. Nancy Adler of McGill University said in an article entitled "The Arts & Leadership: Now That We Can Do Anything, What Will We Do?" published in the *Academy of Management Learning & Education*:

> Constant intuition-based innovation is required to respond to discontinuous change: without it, no business can succeed in the 21st century... As the business environment more frequently calls upon managers to respond to unpredicted and unpredictable threats and opportunities, the ability to improvise increasingly determines organizations' effectiveness. Managers and management students don't understand how to create on cue, how to innovate reliably on a deadline...nor have they developed team-based collaborative skills.

I have a dear friend who recently said his life is an amusement park. One day, it is a roller coaster, and the next, it is a fun house. This is a perfect analogy of the instability in government and business throughout the world today due to the discontinuous change we experience daily. A leader is only as effective as the foundation they have built that allows the leader both to determine what is real or a distortion of the truth and to weather the ups and downs of organizational change. This foundation provides balance not only to the leader, but also to the leader's team and other followers.

Several years ago, I was involved in an unprecedented act of courage by an organization typically run in a fairly totalitarian manner from the top down. By this, I mean that decisions were normally made by the senior management team and treated as if they were law, with no room for input. The act of courage that happened was an attempt to step away from that leadership model to *create* change that would pull a division of a Fortune 100 company from the bottom 25th percentile to the top-most layer in comparison with their direct competitors, improving processing time to directly affect the bottom line.

> A team was created drawing people from all parts of the organization. Widely different skill sets and strengths were pulled in, along with an uncommon mix of decision-making authority, from various physical locations within the United States. The assignment was to work together as a team for as long as it took to redefine the company's way of doing business, and to set the priorities for implementation. To accomplish this seemingly impossible task, each person on the team had to take a leadership role.

> The first hurdle the team had to overcome was trust, not only in themselves, but also in the stated goal and in the people leading the team. The culture of the organization had not previously been conducive to the relationships required for this team to be successful, so the appointment of leadership was critical from the very beginning. The precedent had to be set as the team was pulled together, and previous ways of behavior needed to be left behind. A foundation of leadership for the team was absolutely necessary.

The character traits of trust, authenticity, empathy, compassion, courage, vulnerability and humility all contribute to the balance that this foundation of leadership provides. These character traits are what you bring to the conversation, which creates the relationships necessary to effect change. In times of transformation, the conversations we have must be fierce. Fierce conversations are defined by Susan Scott as "robust, intense, strong, powerful, passionate, eager, unbridled, uncurbed, untamed: one in which we come out from behind ourselves into the conversation and make it real." It is only through fierce conversations that we are able to keep our spirits present so we might discover what is real by listening, asking, mirroring and reflecting back to people what you have heard. In doing so, you will help them feel seen, understood and felt, laying the groundwork of trust.

Drawing people to you by building a balanced foundation of leadership and trust, you will become skilled at connecting individuals and teams in collaborative debates that question what is real. You will inspire and encourage stimulated discussion around creating clear goals. You will also find yourself repeatedly utilizing the knowledge of the many to solve problems, choosing to be creative and flexible in evaluating opportunities and designing strategies. These actions will result in the best possible decisions for the organization that, when implemented, will yield results.

To continue with our example, the first few all day meetings for the team were designed to build relationships. Team members did not jump into a deep discussion of the business model, but spent time talking about their values, their personal and professional visions for themselves, their families, and their successes *and* failures. They shared their personality types and characteristics, and talked about how best to communicate with them, and how they best communicated. Members of the team spent time listening and practicing empathy and compassion. These exercises required people to be authentically who they were and to be vulnerable.

> The interesting part was that as people began to know and understand each other, the joy of being together began to be palpable. They were excited to be working together, and to learn from each other. It also allowed them to be able to manage themselves, to be able to respectfully call a peer out when he or she were slipping back into behavior that was not conducive to the level of commitment they were making to each other, and to celebrate breakthroughs in relationships the likes of which they had not experienced before within the organization.

Personal Responsibility

This leads us to the second principle of Character-Based Leadership, *personal responsibility*. Personal responsibility shows up in our daily actions. It shows in the leader's ability to be accountable and disciplined in the implementation of the mission and values of the organization. For this to occur as a leader, your own values must mesh with the organization, creating the motivation to succeed.

> *For true change, we must accept our personal responsibility to move beyond fear, selfishness and superiority to a place of deep understanding and care for the benefit of all.* ~ ***Maureen Simon***, *"Personal Responsibility in Leadership Serves All"*

The principle of personal responsibility requires you to build your skills in delegation, in all directions. In doing so, you must hold conversations with peers, followers and those you are following. These conversations will create clarity around responsibilities and raise the level of collective accountability and, subsequently, personal accountability. Through the give and take of compassionate conversation combined with the goal of understanding the individual journeys being taken by all members of the organization, each person will understand their path of development. They will know that it is their responsibility to ensure that development happens with help, wherever it is needed, through coaching and mentorship. Action plans are developed and implemented on time and on budget. Goals are achieved, and success is celebrated. This level of accountability frees everyone, including the leader, to take on more multifaceted levels of responsibility.

More importantly, personal responsibility requires reality to be interrogated, especially when things go awry. It requires each team member to recognize their part in the collective process and to never seek to shift blame. The beauty of this aspect of Character-Based Leadership is that the leader is a member of the team and is also held accountable for their actions by the team, creating a culture of collective responsibility that is as strong as the individual levels of personal integrity.

As our team began to shape and define the work necessary to accomplish their goals, they began to assign themselves to smaller breakout teams based upon their learned skills, but also upon their strengths and gifts, and the knowledge they brought of the companies they represented within the overarching division of the corporation. The breakout teams set up a meeting structure that allowed them to return to their previous assignments periodically. There they began the in-depth conversations required to gain deep understanding of the thoughts, ideas, and reasoning around the core values and mission of their operational division, and how that translated into a way of doing business. They pulled together mini-teams from all levels of the organization and asked members to research, document and report back their findings. They then came physically back into the fold of their breakout teams, and ultimately the central team, to report, brainstorm and innovate.

Leaders who make it a practice to draw out the thoughts and ideas of their subordinates (peers and superiors) and who are receptive even to bad news will be properly informed. Communicate downward to subordinates with at least the same care and attention as you communicate upward to superiors. ~ L. B. Belker

This coming together as a central team proved to be difficult. The findings that came out of the research led to some very complicated and thorny issues. The trust that had been built previously needed to be reinforced by each member of the team, including the senior leadership charged with making this process work. Deep feelings were expressed by members who were struggling to honor their personal values, while also honoring the organization's values. Team members wanted to slip into "hallway conversations" instead of sharing their thoughts openly and authentically. This came about because of past history, but more importantly because senior leadership misstepped in several group discussions and shook the foundation that had been laid in previous months. It became obvious that this "experiment" in cultural change had not been completely successful. The leaders of the team did not consider themselves part of the team, and the culture of collective responsibility did not include the top leaders being held accountable by the team.

Climbing over the hurdles created by fear was an arduous task. The hurdles were all over the place and needed to be addressed separately and completely.

1. The fear of repercussion to authentically shared feelings;

2. The fear of change; and

3. The fear of not being liked/loved by people they worked with who were resistant to change.

These hurdles required each member of the team to embrace and live the third principle of Character-Based Leadership, authenticity.

Authenticity

The third principle of Character-Based Leadership, *authenticity*, gives us courage to live our values, declare our priorities, and make the hard decisions. The risk in this is profound. When you risk an authentic conversation, you are exercising the character traits of vulnerability, humility and trust. You risk that *you will be known, you will be seen, and you will be changed*. Authenticity allows you to open yourself to the truth, to see the fun house for what it is, and to step aside and let others lead when they are more qualified to do so. This builds trust and respect, and will transform a company into a great place to work.

One of the outcomes of the work done by the team was to close a physical plant within the division, moving the work to another location thousands of miles away. Since some members of the team were from that location, this was a particularly tough time for them. It required them to disengage from the very deep emotions driving them and to open themselves up to the truth of the situation and the decision. Some were able to do that, but others continued to struggle throughout the entire process. Those able to disengage from their own emotions so that they might deal with the employees of the plant being closed with compassion and understanding were far more successful. Their commitment to the employees being removed from service created trust and respect on both sides of the equation.

One particular gentleman on the team comes to mind as being particularly compassionate and loving, as he delivered termination papers to employees throughout the plant. He amazed me in his ability to create the connections with the employees that were necessary to help them get over the hurdles they faced as they moved on to the next stage of their lives. He was able to do this because he was willing to take the time to listen and have a conversation with each and every one of them, whenever they needed him. He created a connection, a relationship, with every person he talked to. This willingness, perhaps I should say passion, came from his core values of being gentle, compassionate, loving, focused and clear.

Passion

Passion, ah yes, *passion* is our fourth principle. When you are passionate about your vision, your mission, and the values that support the attainment of the goals, and you make that public, it keeps things personal. When you allow—no, encourage—that same passion in your teammates, it creates space for them to act like owners, opening up the creativity to the entrepreneurs hiding within. It guarantees that you and your team stay in the flow created by your customers, the opportunities they give to you, and the vision of your organization. Also, when you are in the flow, projects become easier, collaboration is a way of life, and success becomes a reality.

When you have passion, you stop focusing on activities and begin focusing on action. You and your employees are engaged, change is fluid, priorities are known, and you begin building leadership from the ground up.

Passion is generated when conversations are intense, unbridled and uncurbed. This means there will be disagreements without animosity or tension. It means that everyone gets to share their thoughts and ideas until all have been shared and there is nothing left to say. When all knowledge, skills and creative ideas are on the table, a team built on trust and common purpose—one committed to the vision and the mission—will begin to collaborate in developing a workable and brilliant plan. Your job as the leader is to sit back and let it happen. Your job is to facilitate the conversation as it becomes what it is meant to be. Your job is to ask the hard questions and wait for the answers. This requires you to coach and sometimes to confront. It takes courage and a profound sense of self.

> When top leadership within our example began to let all members of the team do their jobs based on their passion and share their thoughts and ideas, trust began to be restored. Work that was not being shared had begun within breakout teams, and often, those teams had operated at cross-purposes. Hard questions were asked and answered. Many hours of coaching took place, and several times, members of the team confronted each other, asking for more authenticity, more openness, and more honesty. When those barriers were broken down, collaboration within the central team was once again restored. The work flowed more easily, with fewer rough patches between team members, and between team members and leaders.

Service

The final principal of *service* forms the spirit of what it means to be an individual or a team operating in a culture of collective responsibility. This service is not motivated out of self-interest, but out of a commitment to do what is best for everyone. This principle ensures that the heart of the organization beats strongly in service to its purpose. Leaders who hold the character trait of service in high regard are respected. Employees, customers and other leaders look to them for guidance in times of uncertainty, chaos, fortune and misfortune.

> *"The less people know, the more they yell."*
> ~ Seth Godin

Michael McKinney, in his article "Choosing Service Over Self-Interest: The Focus of Leadership," from Leadership Now, writes:

> In the context of what Mr. Lippmann [American newspaper commentator] is talking about, [leadership] means not only maintaining the vision of and faith in those ideals, beliefs and hopes, but living those values as a model and example for others

to follow. It means raising the sights and holding the focus of those we lead such that they are empowered to reach their potentials. It means enabling people by getting the roadblocks out of their way and often out of their thinking. To do this, of course, the leader must grasp the larger picture at all times and hold the course for the benefit of all.

In other words, leadership is a state of being; it is who the leader is, and it is reflected in the leader's conversations. It may not always be popular, but it will create respect.

What was the outcome of the goal laid in front of our team? The larger picture was reached, at least in part, with significant change to the way business was done, and with benefits numbering in the millions of dollars to the bottom line. Several major projects came about because of the work done by the team. Many were extremely successful; others were not. The success was driven by the level of leadership skills exercised as each project commenced and progressed. Those projects led by leaders who learned from the attempt to change the overarching corporate culture were successful. Those projects led by leaders more interested in politics and self-preservation were doomed to embarrassing and expensive failure.

More importantly, the relationships forged by members of the team have been enduring and profoundly heartfelt. Team members have gone on to pursue their life interests, and most have remembered the valuable lessons they learned just by practicing the language of leadership: creating relationships through conversation.

Remembering that *the conversation is the relationship* and employing that concept as you lead with character will bring many benefits to you and to your organization. Let's start with these:

- Priorities are known by you and your team, helping to prevent the stress of being overwhelmed as a leader.
- Leadership will be grown from the ground up, providing an opportunity for solid succession planning.
- Collective responsibility will produce shared standards of performance and accountability. Mediocrity will become a thing of the past.

- Enthusiasm for flexibility and agility in change environments will keep you "in the flow."
- You will see an eagerness for continued learning; your teammates will become "ah-ha junkies."
- Employees will be happy, productive and engaged in the strategic success of the organization.
- Customers will be captured at an emotional level, bringing them back time and time again.
- Collaboration will cross boundaries regularly.
- The financial health of the organization will flourish.

As I look at corporate and political leadership today, I see few I would classify as Character-Based Leaders. It seems as if we are being led overwhelmingly from fear, scarcity and greed for both power and money. The challenge is for those of us who believe strongly in our ability to lead change to make ourselves heard. This requires someone to be the recipient of our message. The only way for us to accomplish this is to first listen carefully to the conversation so we might understand what lies underneath the words and the actions of those we are leading. We can then structure the message in the language that ensures that the people we lead will feel heard, seen, understood and felt—the language of leadership.

Chapter 19

Professional Intimacy: The Key to Become a Sustainable Leader

Christina D. Haxton, MA, LMFT

Leadership Defined

If you have been in a leadership role for more than ten years, you might agree that the leadership style you had when you began is different than your leadership style today. How you define leadership has probably changed since then, too. Since there are an infinite number of ways to define leadership, I will use the definition developed by Kevin Cashman in *Leadership from the Inside Out*: "Leadership is authentic influence that creates value."

Cashman looked at the fundamental characteristics of the most effective, results-producing leaders, despite the wide variety of their leadership styles. Three patterns became clear:

1. *Authenticity*: Well-developed self-awareness that openly faces strengths, vulnerabilities and development challenges.
2. *Influence*: Meaningful communication that connects with people by reminding self and others what is genuinely important.
3. *Value Creation*: Passion and aspiration to serve multiple constituencies (self, team, organization, world, family, community) to sustain performance and contribution over the long-term.

Let's take this definition of leadership to a deeper level. What is one characteristic that a leader needs to influence others authentically to create value? Sustainability. Imagine the ripple effect when you throw a rock into a pond. Now imagine that rock is you, a sustainable leader who sees renewal in relationship—green energy, if you like that image—which in turn harnesses potential and recycles positive change throughout your organization. I propose that an essential characteristic of a Character-Based Leader is sustainability.

A sustainable leader:

- is built to last for the long haul mentally, physically and spiritually.
- is developed from the inside out and is continually shaped by those around her, from the outside in.
- recognizes the value of relationships as a dynamic process that has far-reaching influence to drive positive and lasting change within individuals, within teams, and throughout the organization.
- is a product of a dynamic, complex interrelationship between himself and people he interacts with daily.

Although this sounds simple enough, it is not easy to appreciate without a short trip down the memory lane of leadership training.

The Failure of Old-School Leadership Training

Taking the Human out of the Equation

It was not that long ago when teaching "soft skills" (i.e., people skills of communication and interpersonal relationships) was scoffed at by people who made the training decisions. Why was this? Was it because the ROI of soft-skills training was not measurable? Was this because we were not sure what skills to measure? Or did people skills really not matter? Probably all of the above. Prior to the globalization of our economy, the 24/7 work environment, the internet, and the speed with which we exchange information, we got by with leaving the human out of the equation. Or did we?

Either way, the tide is turning. The focus on people-driven organizations and leadership agility are the new norm. Thanks to the internet, which facilitates global collaboration across time zones and maps, work that was once performed by individuals is now being tasked to teams who may never even meet across a conference table. The increase in numbers of people who must share information, insights, learning and best practices further stresses communication channels. Leaders today and tomorrow must lead more people at a faster pace than their counterparts of the past. Leaders must also develop trust in people very quickly in order not to lose momentum for the bottom line. It gets even more challenging when you combine that with a more fickle, insecure and transient workforce (research shows that employees don't quit jobs; they quit negative and stressful work environments, and they stay because of positive relationships with their bosses).

So much for ignoring soft skills. Leaders who plan to thrive in a competitive and fast-paced marketplace must first successfully and effectively manage interpersonal relationships. Leadership is not just about top-down influence of others, as many old-school definitions presume. A leader is an integral part of a system of people connected and driven by relationships, good, bad and ugly. Failure to recognize the power of relationships can result in organizational disaster: dissatisfaction, disengagement and dead weight (for the employees *and* the leader!).

In an informal survey of 25 C-suite executive leaders from across industries, leaders were asked the following questions:

> *Leaders who plan to thrive in a competitive and fast-paced marketplace must first successfully and effectively manage interpersonal relationships.*

1. What challenges are you having right now that are critical for you to solve?
2. What one skill or trait do you wish you had had prior to taking your executive position?

The responses overwhelmingly pointed to the human side of the business equation: emotions and behavior. More than 90% reported that their previous leadership training program failed in the area of developing the interpersonal skills necessary for their leadership roles. Leaders felt ill-equipped to resolve conflict and to effectively communicate with their new teams.

In the survey, respondents were asked to describe the challenges that currently kept them awake at night. Their answers are summarized below and reflected the leaders' observation of the problems facing the teams for which he or she had no effective solutions:

- Low team morale or burnout
- Role confusion among team members
- Conflict avoidance and unresolved issues
- Lack of creativity, inspiration and productivity
- Ineffective or toxic communication among the team or from one member

In retrospect, these leaders identified many fail points in their past or current leadership training:

- "Leadership training focused on developing competencies, yet competencies felt irrelevant because they were not tied to success in my specific goals or role in my company."
- "I knew I needed to learn how to quickly get my new team on board, but I needed buy-in from my boss and didn't want to look incompetent, so I didn't ask."
- "I can only get training approved if it is results-focused, improves the bottom line, and is clearly measurable (ROI). Since 'soft skills' were not 'measurable,' my organization will not support it."
- "Any benefits of the annual executive leadership retreat fade after the first week. There is no follow-through or accountability. Then we are back to the 'same old habits' and nothing changes back at work."
- "The last leadership training I attended espoused treating people as tools, drones, to be told what to do and how to do it, reflecting a 'you're not paid to think' mentality, which is clearly not the case in business today."
- "I was not offered any opportunities for building my leadership skills once I was promoted to Senior VP. My boss believed that trust and respect by my team should be automatic and came with my title. It would have been nice if all of the team got the memo."
- "The belief was that soft skills were fluffy and could not be measured and not worth investing in. Upper management did not have a clue how to build or grow human capital and its requirement for organizational success. Any training having to

do with our people skills like emotion, beliefs and values was ignored. I no longer work there and am happier for it."

The writing on the wall is clear: the burn-out and burn-up rate for newly promoted or hired executives is astounding, with almost 50% of newly hired or newly promoted executives quitting or getting fired before their 18-month anniversary. Research shows the majority of executives failed because of their attitudes, which included a lack of emotional mastery, interpersonal skills or stress resulting in physical burn-out.

Although there have been great strides in leadership development in the past 30 years, there continues to be a disconnect between the leadership training solutions offered by organizations and what leaders need to nurture the human side of the leadership equation. Leadership strategies based on outdated definitions of leadership continue to need updating. Leaders who close the gap between what is known to inspire and motivate people and what they are actually *doing* in their day-to-day conversations and actions will be built to last. Sustainable leaders will have the interpersonal and communication skills to close this gap.

The Powerful Dynamic among the "You," the "I," and the "We" of Effective Leadership

Here's where brain science meets business strategy: High emotional intelligence (EQ) is the best predictor of success for leaders. Daniel Goleman's work on emotional intelligence precisely identified this inner-outer and outer-inner dynamic as the two interactive qualities of emotional intelligence: awareness of self and awareness of others. Recent advances in neuroscience show us what really motivates people and what makes great leaders great. Finally, we can link a leader's soft skills to the bottom line! Goleman's research points to emotional intelligence as a critical ingredient to leadership effectiveness and success.

But wait, there's more! Let's not forget the power of the relationships that are created in the process. Those relationships make up the life and breath of the organization. The art and science of communication is three dimensional: $1(I) + 1(you) = 3(we)$. Imagine what happens when you throw a rock into a pond. Ripples flow not only visibly across the surface, but also throughout the entire body of water. Understanding yourself, other people and the power of the resulting relationships is only the beginning. Going from understanding into action is the key to your leadership success, and now becomes your personal leadership challenge.

On your mark... Get set... GO! With everything else you are juggling, how can you create positive lasting change and build resilience in your team, support complex human interactions, help people embrace conflict, build trust to retain valuable employees, be able to adapt, and yet be flexible enough to change at the speed of light while continuing to focus on the business's bottom line? Whew! That tall order calls for a little conversation about intimacy. No, not *the talk* about the birds and the bees you had with your teenager, but *professional intimacy.*

Professional Intimacy: What Is It?

As a coach and a marriage counselor for more than 15 years, I have often said to myself, "If only my clients knew what I know about what motivates people and how to communicate effectively, then they could solve their problems quickly and fire me sooner!" I began to teach my clients what I had been trained to do as a therapist to show them how to make lasting positive change in themselves and to solve their relationship problems for good. Since we spend more time at work than at home, I had them practice the skills at work first. Practice makes perfect, and your brain does not care who you are practicing on. The results at home were great. What I didn't expect to hear were the surprising results people were getting at work (after all, it was just supposed to be practice!). *Professional intimacy* was born.

Beyond *emotional intelligence* (understanding your needs and what motivates you) and *social intelligence* (understanding and attending to the needs of others) lies the practice of *professional intimacy*. Wait, it is not what you think! A leader who learns and practices the skills of professional intimacy sees the *relationship* as the platform upon which he develops his own characteristic of sustainability. This leader not only strives to develop himself personally, but also assists others in facilitating their own unique creativity and solutions. Remember the ripples in the pond?

And here's a BONUS: The positive ripple effect of communicating with compassion is felt by the listener as well as by the leader *and* builds trust. Richard Boyatzis's research on the positive physiological effects of compassion as a direct result of coaching others proves to reduce "power stress," a unique stress experienced by leaders. Ignore the effects of power stress and you are headed for physical burn-up, mental burn-out, or both.

Professional intimacy is a three-step, value-driven process in which a leader (or anyone who is in a position to authentically influence others to create value) can become more sustainable, become more resilient, and build trust in the process of building a successful business:

1. ***Know thyself.*** Leaders can ask and answer the following questions to develop intrapersonal awareness and clarity: *Who am I? Where am I going? Why am I going there?* Reflective questions build your EQ, or the "emotional and social intelligence muscles" in your brain. Take the time to reflect on what you learn about yourself from successes and mistakes. Remember, practice makes perfect and creates habits.

2. ***Seek to understand others.*** Neurologically and physiologically, the very same brain chemicals that are responsible for us feeling fear are also present when we feel curious. Fear is contagious, but fear can also be "felt" by others, which is experienced as dissonance, otherwise known as stress or anxiety. The only difference between me feeling fear and me feeling curiosity is how I explain the situation to myself, which may be inside of or outside of my awareness. When you are curious rather than defensive (fear) and are willing to listen to others at a deeper level, the conversation becomes a way to make a positive connection at a personal and emotional level. This is experienced as caring, which inspires hope, connection and resilience in others. It is this skill of interpersonal attunement and communication that affords you as a leader the greatest opportunity to make a difference in your day-to-day interactions with others.

3. ***See relationships as opportunities.*** In relationships, we learn and grow, and in conversation, we create reality for ourselves and others. Here is your opportunity to build trust and create a

strong relationship that is the key ingredient to facilitating positive change, inspiring creativity, and fueling internal motivation in people. Every conversation is an opportunity to learn and grow, which is the ultimate brain candy.

Since we spend more time at work than we do at home, and because we need to practice new skills when the costs are low, I encouraged my clients to practice new communication skills with people at work before they tried those skills at home with their partners or teenagers. The relationship was the litmus test for my clients. Their homework was to be aware of and to simply observe their own internal responses and the responses of the other people when they made simple changes in their language in the face of potential conflicts. I have used this approach in my family and marital therapy practice for many years and have taught clients how to use similar solutions with their work teams and organizations with positive and lasting results.

What Does Professional Intimacy Look Like in a Simple Conversation?

When you understand how the human brain works, along with all of its strengths and limitations, you can build your sustainability muscle in simple, brief conversations. The best opportunities for this are when there is conflict. But first, you will appreciate a few facts about how your brain works when it comes to conflict.

Just for a moment, imagine the following scenario:

Remember your last argument? Neither of you remember how it started or what it was about and, before you know it, it's off to the races! About 20 minutes later, a great comeback pops into your head. *Aha! I wish I would have said that instead. Why couldn't I think of that at the time?*

Due to the hard-wiring in our brains, the *lizard brain*, managing our emotions can be harder than we think. Here's a little explanation why and three simple steps to stay cool under pressure the next time the lizard threatens to hijack your brain.

A complaining customer, an out-of-control employee, or an irate boss can at some point, cause you to lose your cool. People push our buttons, and we feel irritated, frustrated, and overwhelmed, and sometimes we just explode. Or we hold it in, tell ourselves it's no big deal, it doesn't matter what we do, it won't make a difference what we say, so we say nothing and pretend it's okay and march on, which is a recipe for stress-related disease. Either way, we feel regret, shame and humiliation at how we've just lost our tempers again. Here come the "should haves." *I should've known better, stayed calm, counted to ten, remembered what happened last time I lost my temper.* Lizard brain makes it impossible to act on the should-haves. Here's why.

Lizard Brain

In many ways, the human brain has evolved since we were cave dwellers. Humans have complex language, use tools to make and fix things, and send people into outer space. The part of the brain responsible for survival, the amygdala, an almond-shaped area at the base of the brain, way down deep and part of the limbic system, otherwise known as "fight or flight central," still exists, however, even though we are no longer running from saber-toothed cats.

In response to stress, the limbic system goes into high gear and the fight, flight or freeze response gets activated. It's automatic, and there's no thought involved. Triggers might be his or her yelling or icy stare and can often include what I call "universal lizard-brain words" such as *Why did you ...? You always...! You never ...! You should... No!* (Hands on hips, finger-wagging, and eye-rolling are optional.)

The limbic system has been triggered, and the lizard brain is now in charge. We feel emotionally hijacked, and the "thinking brain" is rendered helpless. These triggers can bring up strong emotions (e.g., pain) from the past right into the present moment, as if it's happening all over again. The lizard's primary responsibility is to protect us from perceived harm. The lizard has now jumped into the driver's seat and we are in the back, a passenger hanging on for dear life, yet the road is oddly, comfortably familiar.

Congratulations, You Are Human

So, how is it that lizard brain happens repeatedly to highly intelligent people? It's not about IQ or an inability to learn from past mistakes. It's just the default wiring of our very human brains.

The lizard brain switches off the thinking brain, or the prefrontal cortex, where reasoning and understanding happen, which explains why your *aha!* moment after an argument comes later, probably after a few deep, belly breaths when the reactive lizard brain is no longer driving the bus and the pre-frontal cortex receives the oxygen it needs to regain control. It's a myth that if we understand why we react, we will automatically be able to respond calmly next time our buttons get triggered. The rational pre-frontal cortex can't always prevent the lizard brain from engaging. The pre-frontal cortex is out-powered and just not that evolved. It is impossible to not feel a feeling. It's not caused by a weakness, just wiring, so stop trying.

What's the good news? The good news comes from recent scientific discoveries that our brains aren't hard and set like concrete at age three, which is what neuroscientists (brain researchers) believed until very recently. Neuroplasticity is the good news. Our brains can and do make new connections and build new neural pathways by the millions every day, most of which we are not even aware of... Scary.

So, changing your habits, or creating new neural pathways, is actually quite simple (I said simple, not easy), even if habits have been around for years.

First, pick one person or situation that triggers your lizard (it won't be hard; family gives us ample opportunity to practice). Begin by simply noticing opportunities to recognize your lizard brain as it creeps up on you, or identify situations in which your lizard brain gets triggered.

Next, we're going to create a new habit or neural pathway.

Three Simple Steps to Stay Cool under Pressure: Notice, Acknowledge and Rename

1. *Notice the pattern.* Simply become an observer of the pattern, as if you are watching from the sidelines. What has to happen to

trigger your own, your partner's, or your boss's lizard brain? Describe the pattern sequence to yourself or someone else. Do you react to lizard brain words? If so, which ones? Do you use them with others? Notice what happens when you replace a judgmental *Why did you ...?* with a sincere question. For instance, *How do you see it?* When asked with genuine curiosity, words such as "what" and "how" land differently than "why" and allow you to create more productive pathways in your brain (and his or her brain).

2. ***Acknowledge the emotion.*** Use your powers of observation without judgment (ban the should-haves). Notice the opportunity to acknowledge the emotion without feeling you "should" change it, stop it, or judge it as bad or wrong. Instead, see what happens when you respond with an emotion such as curiosity and words such as "Mmm, interesting …" (with your eyebrows up, please!). See if you can get a little distance and prevent an emotional hijack by observing the conversation as if you were a bystander.

3. ***Rename the feeling.*** Label or rename the feeling (not the person, not the person's motivation, not the person's intention) as sad, scared, or hurt instead of angry. Anger is not a primary emotion, but a secondary emotion, a "safer" feeling, and often hides primary emotions such as sadness, fear or pain. When we believe someone is angry, the lizard brain gets activated and we can feel defensive. When we can re-label anger as sadness, fear, pain, or a combination of those feelings, the part of the brain responsible for empathy is engaged. The lizard can get out of the driver's seat and the thinking brain can work again.

Practice makes perfect and new neural pathways. Changing behavior or learning to do something new takes awareness, intention, action and practice, just like when you learned to ski, ride a bike, or play the guitar. There's no way around it. By understanding a few simple facts about how our brains work and making small adjustments to the words we use and practice (yes, even imagining yourself taking these steps will create new neural pathways, because the brain doesn't know the difference between what's imagined and what's real), we can stay cool under pressure, lower blood pressure, and, as crazy as it sounds, begin to see conflict as an opportunity for practice and a little fun, too.

The Effect of the Sustainable Leader

Kevin Cashman states, "Leadership does not exist in a vacuum. It always operates in context, in relationship. While leaders may lead by virtue of who they are, leaders also create value by virtue of their relationships."

Imagine yourself as a sustainable leader who is built to last not just for today, but also for whatever tomorrow will bring. Imagine the difference between being a leader who feels satisfied, happy and purposeful, who has a successful, thriving organization and leaves a legacy to be carried on by sustainable successors... and being a leader who burns out and burns up.

As a sustainable leader who sees every conversation as an opportunity to learn and grow, you will find that your personal and professional life will feel more satisfying, rewarding and balanced. As a sustainable leader, you recognize that time is a limited resource. Since you practice professional intimacy, you feel re-energized and re-charged at the end of the day. You get more done in less time and are a more effective leader of your organization. Your bottom line is evidence that you build human capital by developing others to develop yourself. What began as a ripple effect is now a powerful tsunami throughout your organization and beyond.

Part IV

Leadership Communities

Chapter 20

Becoming a Better Leader through a Community Assessment

Chapter 21

Social Media Communities as the Laboratory for Leaders

Chapter 20

Becoming a Better Leader through a Community Assessment

Will Lukang

Oprah captures the true meaning of being authentic. Authentic is being true to yourself and doing the right thing no matter what the circumstances. The word "authentic" also implies being trustworthy and acting according to one's belief and core values. It means someone is genuine. Character-Based Leaders start from a foundation of being authentic.

When thinking of authentic leadership, there are two key attributes that come to mind, *integrity* and *trust*. How well a Character-Based Leader exemplifies those traits comes from

> *"Real integrity is doing the right thing, knowing that nobody's going to know whether you did it or not."*
> ~ *Oprah Winfrey*

three personal components: values, strengths and skills. The combination of these three elements defines the person, which determines the person's level of integrity and trust.

Throughout this book, you have been exposed to many ideas about what a Character-Based Leader is and how to develop into a better one. Clearly, integrity and trust have been mentioned repeatedly in these discussions, along with the concept of being authentic. But how does a leader successfully raise the bar to become a Character-Based Leader and continue beyond that to realize even higher levels of effectiveness?

Several chapters in this book include ways to evaluate yourself and to set goals for improvement. Following the ideas presented would be an excellent first step to start your own leadership development. To really hone ourselves into full-blown Character-Based Leaders, however, we need feedback from those we work with. Leadership is not done alone. It's about how we interact with others. It's about how willing others are to follow our direction and to embrace a common vision.

Only by receiving objective evaluations of our roles as leaders from others can we grow into the leaders we really want to be. What follows is the kernel of an idea you can expand on to make this happen. It's called a "360° Character-Based Leadership Assessment." Experiment with it, alter it, add to it, and see how it can help you grow into the leader you want to be. Then share your experiences with others in the Lead Change Group so this tool can be further refined to help more leaders become Character-Based Leaders.

Why an Assessment?

The purpose of the assessment is to provide a bird's-eye view as to how well someone leads. It also provides a baseline, or a starting point, to create action plans that could help a leader become more effective. One might argue that an assessment could be inaccurate. This is only a tool to help us grow. It is up to us to interpret the results for our own growth. The main purpose of this assessment is to help a leader become more self-aware. In that regard, it is a development tool more than a certificate of authenticity. When we become aware of how others view our levels of authenticity, our integrity, and our ability to engender trust, we will know what we need to do to become better leaders.

The assessment would be conducted as a 360° review. In a business or organizational setting, the participants include peers, subordinates, mentors, immediate managers, and other stakeholders. However, the same assessment can be used in any form of community, even the family unit, where "peers" are spouses, "subordinates" are children, and so on. Throughout the rest of this chapter though, let's assume the assessment it being conducted in a business or organizational setting.

The reason for a 360° review is to provide an overall perspective from the vantage points of those we interact with most. The main objective is to help the leader grow and develop into a better leader. The assessment is only a tool. This tool works when leaders have the desire to further improve themselves for the welfare of their constituents and organizations.

Selection of Participants

It is important to note that the leader is at the center of the process and that the assessment is conducted to help the leader improve. The leader therefore selects those individuals within the organization who are best suited to provide an accurate assessment of his or her skills.

During this process, the key stakeholders are the leader's manager or managers (in a matrix organization), peers whom the leader interacts with daily, and the leader's direct reports. The direct reports are the ones who know and understand the leader's behavior because they have the most interaction with the leader.

In the selection phase, it is important to involve as many direct reports as possible to create an accurate assessment of the leader's behavior.

The Assessment Process

The assessment flow chart below describes how the assessment will be conducted. It provides the steps for the 360° Character-Based Leadership Assessment and details for each of the steps.

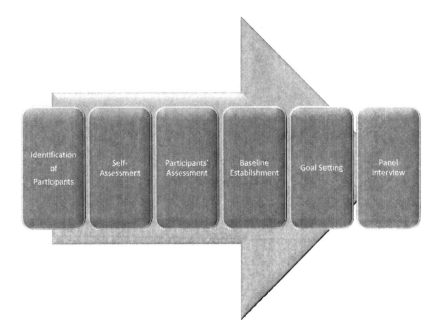

It's important to note that the 360° assessment is an iterative process. As you complete the assessment and apply the knowledge you have gained from it, it's worthwhile to come back later and do the assessment again. Each time you go through the process, new areas for improvement will be identified, enabling you to become the best leader possible through the help and feedback of your community.

Identification of Participants

The identification of participants is a critical step in the process. A lopsided distribution of participants would skew the results of the assessment. It is important to make sure that at least half of the direct reports are included in the assessment. It is equally important to make sure that the leader's manager is also involved, because a leader's behavior can vary depending on whom he or she interacts with.

Self-Assessment

The self-assessment by the leader provides a bird's-eye view of how the leader perceives him- or herself. What follows are some questions a leader should reflect on during this self-assessment. Other questions could be added to this, if desired.

- Give an example of a situation in which you had to assume a leadership role. How might you have improved the way you handled it?
- What's the best way to describe your career progression?
- What's the best way to describe the work atmosphere of your team?
- Describe a situation in which you fought for your team. What was the situation? Why did you fight?
- Have you allowed your team to make an important decision on its own? Why? What were the results? How do you feel about what happened?
- Will you do the right thing regardless of whether anyone is looking? Are there any circumstances in which you might not?
- What would you do if you realized you made a mistake and revealing it would cause serious repercussions?
- Have you been in a situation in which you had to announce a painful decision and tried to minimize how serious this was? Why did you do this? How did it turn out?
- If you were given an opportunity to get promoted, but had to bend the rules to make it happen, would you do it? Why?
- Have you encountered a situation in which you had to choose between making the right decision or pleasing a supervisor? What happened? Why did you make this choice?
- How often do you seek your constituents' feedback? Under what circumstances would you make a decision without involving them? Why?
- Are there any circumstances you have encountered in which honesty was not the best way to handle the situation? Why?
- On a scale of 1 to 10, with 10 being the highest, how would your direct reports rate you on the following leadership traits:
  - You are authentic in the way you conduct yourself.
  - You are a person of the highest integrity.

- You can be trusted to do the right thing and lead the team in the right direction.

Participants' Assessments

The participants' assessment is the step that involves and engages the participants in providing a fair evaluation of a leader. It is important to get their buy-in to do the assessment in a timely manner. It is also worth pointing out that their assessments would be anonymous. Here are some of the questions participants should be asked during the assessment:

- Does the leader practice open and honest communication?
  - Never
  - Sometimes
  - Most of the time
  - Always

  Please give an example to illustrate. How did this make you feel?

- Is the leader willing to compromise just to achieve a goal?
  - Never
  - Sometimes
  - Most of the time
  - Always

  Please give an example to illustrate. How did this make you feel?

- Does the leader take the time to explain his or her decision when tough decisions are made?
  - Never
  - Sometimes
  - Most of the time
  - Always

  What happened when the leader had to make a tough decision?

- Does the leader allow the team to make important decisions on its own?

- Never
- Sometimes
- Most of the time
- Always

Share an example of when the leader did this or when you felt the leader should have done this.

- Does the leader treat everyone in the same way?
  - Never
  - Sometimes
  - Most of the time
  - Always

Describe some situations that illustrate how the leader treats different people.

- Does the leader do favors in exchange for something?
  - Never
  - Sometimes
  - Most of the time
  - Always

Share an example when this happened and how you feel about it.

- Does the leader seek out and listen to everyone's feedback?
  - Never
  - Sometimes
  - Most of the time
  - Always

Describe a situation to illustrate this, including how it affected the team and the results.

- Do you think the leader will do the right thing regardless of whether anyone is looking?
- Do you think your leader would tell you if he or she made a mistake?
- What's your level of confidence in your leader's decisions and directions?
- If you have a choice, would you continue to work with this leader? Please explain.

- Describe a situation in which the leader fought for the team. What was the situation? What are your feelings about this?
- What's the best way to describe the work atmosphere of your team?
- Do you think the leader would bend the rules to get ahead?
- On a scale of 1 to 10, with 10 being the highest, how would you rate the leader on the following leadership traits:
  - The leader is authentic in the way they conduct themselves.
  - The leader is a person of the highest integrity.
  - The leader can be trusted to do the right thing and to lead the team in the right direction.

Baseline Establishment

Once the assessments are completed, the next step is setting a baseline based on the answers provided by the participants versus those provided by the leader. The result of this step is a comparison of the perception of the leader to the perception of the participants. The establishment of the baseline forms the foundation for the goal-setting step as well as a benchmark to look back on the next time this assessment is done.

Goal Setting

During the goal-setting step, the leader creates actionable items that should follow the SMART principle to ensure that the leader's development program is meaningful. SMART means the goal must be Specific, Measurable, Actionable, Realistic and Time-bound. The leader can complete this step alone, with a manager, or working with an optional panel of experts. This assessment process is flexible enough to be used by individual leaders or adopted by an entire organization.

Panel Interview

The panel interview is an optional element that can be incorporated into the assessment. It would be conducted by individuals who are experts in Character-Based Leadership, not participants. This additional step offers the view of third-party, objective outsiders who do not work inside the organization and who have no direct working relationship with the leader who is being evaluated. They would review the self-assessment, participants' assessments, baseline analysis, and SMART goals, then conduct an interview of the leader based on their findings. Finally, they would share recommendations for how the leader can develop skills for the next level.

A Commitment to Change

Becoming a Character-Based Leader starts with a commitment. It is a commitment to change and improvement. It is a commitment to hold oneself to a higher standard. It is a commitment to never stop growing and learning. It is a commitment to authenticity, integrity and trust-building. This requires feedback from those you lead and from those you work with and for. The 360° Character-Based Leadership Assessment is just one tool in the toolkit you'll develop as you seek to strengthen your Character-Based Leadership skills; however, it should be viewed as an indispensible tool to accomplish this goal and to help increase the number of leaders aspiring to reach a higher level of effectiveness.

Chapter 21

Social Media Communities as the Laboratory for Leaders

Meghan M. Biro

As leaders, we live in a Web economy. Most of us do, at any rate. Nearly all who are in the workforce or are attempting to join the workforce look to the Web first. As leaders, we must be aware of this bias as we search online for employees. We know that prospective employees are researching to see who they know at various companies, even as we search for their connections and affiliations. The teams we lead rely on the Web and on social media to understand and support our brands.

As employees search online for validation of our organizations, they use the Web to determine if an employer's brand is consistent with their values and personal brand. This means we, as leaders, must be sure that our brands are healthy and correctly position the cultures of our companies. We must anticipate that potential

> *Social media and online communities are essential workplace and leadership tools.*

employees are researching our management and leadership teams online to get a sense of the workplace's culture and ethics, even as we must accept that our teams are using the Web and social media to gauge our performance as leaders. It is a relentless cycle, and leaders must stay one step ahead.

Searching online and having a credible presence online is not enough in a Web economy, however. Social media and its many communities hold the key to success in understanding where workplace culture and leadership stand today.

Facebook and LinkedIn, early entrants in the community-building business, are almost old-school in their approaches. Facebook attempts to forge communities based on friendship, family ties or "likeness." LinkedIn uses the loose bonds of employment history, education and job specialty to create a nominal community and then presents users with the opportunity to join more tailored communities of interest. Twitter, with its manic free-for-all of seemingly random thoughts, may not seem like the ideal community-building platform, yet communities spring up rapidly and grow quickly, even when constrained to 140 characters. Google+, in its early days, appears to be attempting to trump all others. Time will tell which will lead, but for now, participation in one or more social communities is a necessary leadership skill.

The central lesson is that social media and online communities are essential workplace and leadership tools. If the Web is an ocean, social media and its many communities of interest are the deep, fast current that will enable the leaders of companies to innovate and lead in real time.

Online Social Communities and Trust

Building a social community online is a long-term effort. As Chris Brogan, Paul Gillin, and other social-media luminaries have observed, some online people and communities have more influence than others, largely because they are trusted entities. Influence is the gold standard of online currency. As with all currencies, influence must be present in vast quantities before it is actually needed, and its value can change quickly if a hint of falsity or manipulation emerges.

In a Web economy, *trust* is equivalent in value to *influence*, and both are driven by *intent*. In social communities, intent is more than interest and more than commitment; it's the engine of the community, because people come to communities with a purpose. They are looking for places to be, places to learn, and places to grow and interact, and they come with the intent to realize those goals. Leaders of companies, therefore, must participate in social communities.

Thus, social communities are more than communities of shared interests or loose bonds. They are communities of intent. Social communities gather people with many different personalities, personal brands, goals, aspirations, skill sets and attributes. They are multi-generational, multicultural and global. They allow people of diverse skill sets and temperaments to collaborate and share because they have the intent to collaborate and the social context (a community) in which to realize that intent. It is clear that social communities offer leaders a model for working with employees and for building a culture of leadership.

Creating Communities of Interest and Intent

Let's look at what it takes to build and maintain a powerful social community, and then let's explore the value of that process.

TalentCulture was launched more than two years ago as a social-talent community dedicated to workplace, leadership and talent-recruiting topics. From a core group of fewer than ten trusted contributors (colleagues, peers, and friends), a vibrant social community was knit together slowly. The community's contributors come from diverse backgrounds—IP law, marketing, HR, recruiting, branding, venture capital, career coaching, and leadership consulting. The glue for this diverse group is a passion to create, share and refine the latest perspectives on finding meaningful careers and using them to grow. The community's shared intent is to foster leadership and innovation to create understanding that will lead to better workplaces.

Relationships within the community were deepened as members contributed to blogs on partner websites, commented on each others' blogs, and got together over conference calls. Along the way, contributors posted blogs individually on Facebook and LinkedIn. The socially savvy group also posted links on Twitter, which really got things rolling. Posting links to blogs, posting pointers to other interesting information on workplace, leadership and recruiting trends, and adding various pithy observations on Twitter increased the community's traction, and audience, exponentially.

The next step for many communities of this sort is to progress to a fully social model, which may involve a regular, moderated Twitter chat, commonly referred to as a TweetChat. TweetChat communities typically begin with a group of 40 or so core participants. As word of mouth spreads and trust grows, many groups see the number of participants grow to more than 300 individuals per chat. There is a natural ebb and flow that occurs weekly.

TweetChats or the use of hashtags, like those led by the Lead Change community (#leadchange) and TalentCulture (#tchat) are more than a group of collaborators knocking off 140-character messages on the spur of the moment. The talks must be planned, the moderator (the nominal leader) must do a lot of homework on topics and trends, and participants are given topics, questions and hashtags in advance of the chat. What emerges, however, is not scripted; a recent chat on diversity, for example, avoided the pitfall of discussing stereotypes, gender, age and physical discrimination and instead focused on the much more interesting topic of cognitive diversity, in effect, different yet predictable styles of thinking. One person may have a certain style of thinking; another person, a different style. Depending on differences in styles, the individuals may have trouble understanding and communicating with one another. In the chat on diversity, Joe Gerstandt, a participant and subject matter expert, noted, "Decision making, problem solving and innovation are increasingly important competencies and opportunities for competitive advantage and all of these things are all fed by cognitive diversity."

Of course, cognitive diversity can be difficult to manage. In one instance, a chat participant challenged the community with the comment: "A lot of white people talking up diversity—I don't see a lot of diversity though, just white folks tweeting…"

This could have been a non-recoverable moment, but instead, the community turned it into a leadership moment with a wide range of diverse ideas. Pointing out the cognitive rather than cultural diversity in the group helped put the chat back on track. Social communities can be self-healing systems when trust is built among the participants over time. Various members of my community proposed an analysis of how TweetChats are influencing and laying out the future of online communities, and what that means for leadership. Here are a few notes by Omawale Cassale about these attributes of social communities:

- Collective vs. individual ownership: "When people feel ownership, they become careful stewards of what has been created."
- Participation varies and depends on interest, expertise and willingness to share: "By lowering the barriers of participation, more people are drawn in, which is the key to utilizing the collective knowledge of the community."
- Many popular TweetChats are based on niche topics with the core value proposition being the opportunity to learn more: "Instead of people hoarding knowledge, hashtag chats give participants an opportunity to share their learning with others."
- Heavily focused on crowdsourcing: "Within this dynamic, community participants can ask burning questions that are on their mind [sic] around the subject of interest. This simultaneous loose and rigid structure is especially appealing to participants."

Cassalle further notes:

> In this new dynamic, you have to show your worth in the open community before people will even give you a chance to move into a closed, intimate relationship.

> This dynamic is especially crucial [to master] for employers who are seeking to engage with prospective candidates. By moderating online discussions on subjects related to their industry, company or individual opportunities, leaders can create a dynamic recruiting environment that will be irresistible to candidates.

The message is clear: ignore social communities and you have lost an opportunity with prospective employees to be relevant and to be perceived as a trustworthy leader. Misuse social communities and place your brand reputation, and trust, at risk.

Social Communities as Metaphor for a Culture of Leadership

Why do social communities serve as a metaphor for leadership? Isn't leadership top-down, structured and controlled by employers? Isn't leadership immune to the influence of social media and online communities?

Leadership Communities

While leadership is still in many ways a science, it is also an art. The science part can be taught in business school; the art must either be in a leader's DNA or must be learned and practiced through interchanges with other leaders, employers, HR experts, talent managers, and other subject-matter experts. There is no better laboratory in which to learn the art of leadership than social communities, where thoughts fly fast, groups assemble based on shared interest and intent, and respect is earned, not given. Leaders can actually learn to lead better through social community involvement.

I believe that employers today must know how to use social media to be seen as innovative leaders; respected, trusted brands; and relevant workplaces. Social media and its communities are environments in which leaders can learn to influence, empower, motivate, engage and ultimately lead. They are also a pipeline that will allow leaders to grow their businesses and retain star employees. An added benefit: Through social community involvement, leaders will be better able to attract and draw talent into the pipeline and, ultimately, the workplace.

Creating a social community requires interactions that encompass idealism and pragmatism: Idealism because the intent is to do good things socially through the community, and pragmatism because there must be some return on investment to the community's participants or they won't be engaged in the community (and there will be few opportunities to demonstrate leadership). And, of course, this requires a compelling workplace culture.

Leaders must work into social communities with care. It's essential to observe the culture of the community before moving to interaction. Don't sell, or you'll lose trust and be ignored. Show your leadership stripes by adding value to the discussion. Take the time to consider what others say and to reflect on their contributions. Be a member first, a leader second; in this way your leadership will emerge as an organic and trustworthy attribute and you will be welcomed into the community as a leader.

Welcome to the new world of social communities, where leaders are made, not born.

Part V

Moving Forward

Chapter 22

The Power of Perseverance

Chapter 23

Tomorrow's Leaders

Chapter 22

The Power of Perseverance

Tara R. Alemany

When I was still a teenager, my mother attended a Bill Gothard seminar based on his *Character Sketches* books. This intriguing course looked at different animals, studying their habits and characteristics, and then showed how certain biblical figures modeled the same traits. Excited by all that she had learned, my mother came home and asked each of us in the family what animal we thought we were most like.

As I thought about my answer, I wanted to come up with something majestic and powerful. Wouldn't it be great to be like a lion? I am a classic Leo, after all. Or an eagle, fierce and passionate, noble and powerful? Yes, that'd be a great animal to resonate with. Yet I was embarrassed to admit at the time that the animal whose traits I most nearly resembled was that of a mule.

My life had been filled with challenges that many people I knew had seemingly never had to face. Despite the burden of my particular challenges, I continued to pick one foot up and place it before the other, plodding along, head down, resembling nothing more closely than a mule with a heavy load. More than anything, I recognized that heavy load... I felt it every day.

Fast-forward a number of years. I'm working at a job I love in a temporary capacity, hoping to eventually be hired, when my contract expires and company policies no longer allow further renewal. So, what is there to do next? Thankfully, the company recognized my abilities and didn't want to lose me, but they couldn't hire me due to a hiring freeze. So, my boss contacted a vendor that the company frequently used, and convinced the vendor to hire me so I could come right back into the same position as a contractor. Plodding, plodding, plodding.

A few months later, that vendor had to cut back its staff, and as junior man on the totem pole, my position was eliminated. Recognizing, however, that their client especially wanted me, the vendor asked me to work for them on a freelance basis. The result was the birth of my first company (at the ripe old age of 19), which would be a huge part of my life and career for the next 16 years.

More plodding, plodding, plodding. Or at least that's how I viewed it at the time. My plans to pursue my master's degree and a doctorate and to become a college professor quickly fell by the wayside as I plodded along in a direction I hadn't charted or planned for.

I can't really pinpoint when my thinking changed. Perhaps it was when I had to find my second contract or the third one, but eventually, I saw that there was a difference between plodding and progressing.

Plodding is moving in a direction (usually forward), often with no destination, and frequently at someone else's prompting. *Progressing* is moving forward toward a goal, frequently of our own choosing. One sets a destination, charts the course, and starts taking the necessary steps to reach that destination. It's intentional movement with a purpose and expected outcome.

So, how does this all apply to Character-Based Leadership, and why is it in this book? The experiences of my early life taught me the importance of perseverance, which dictionary.com defines as "steady persistence in a course of action, a purpose, a state, etc. especially in spite of difficulties, obstacles, or discouragement."

As Character-Based Leaders, we know the importance of having a defined objective, of sharing that vision with our followers, and of gaining support and agreement from key stakeholders to accomplish those objectives. But what happens when obstacles arise? Our followers are looking to us to show the way and to lead them to success.

Perseverance or Delusion?

There's perseverance, and then there's just delusion. So, how do we determine which is which, and when do we alter course to avoid delusion?

To begin with, you have to have clear vision as a leader. Keep your eyes focused on the goal and be aware of the obstacles that are likely to arise. This enables you to plan ahead to counter those issues and to continue moving you and your team toward the goal. This is more than just learning from past mistakes, however. It involves conducting what has been dubbed by some as a "premortem."

Author Gary A. Klein, in a Harvard Business Review blog post titled "Performing a Project Premortem," defines a premortem as the hypothetical opposite of a medical postmortem. It comes at the beginning of a project rather than at the end so the project can be improved rather than autopsied. Unlike a typical critiquing session, in which project team members are asked what *might* go wrong, the premortem operates on the assumption that the "patient" has died and asks what *did* go wrong. Often, the team is informed that the project has "died spectacularly." Then, the

> *The Character-Based Leader can only function well within a team when lines of communication remain open.*

team members' task is to generate plausible reasons for the project's failure, and the project manager uses these plausible reasons for failure to strengthen the overall plan. Typical premortems take place after the team has been briefed on the plan, but before any actual work has begun on the project, thus creating a more robust plan that is more likely to have the buy-in of its various team members.

Conducting a premortem to accomplish your goals may help reduce the potential risk in a given course of action, but even more critical than that is ascertaining whether the goal is even worthwhile. There are times when those in management are given a directive that must be filtered down into the organization, but what happens when the directive is counterintuitive or simply wrong?

The Character-Based Leader can function well within a team only when lines of communication remain open and information is shared to the fullest extent allowed. These are facets of an earlier trait discussed in this book, trust. It is important that you, as a Character-Based Leader, have identified the Trust Touchstones of each person on your team and communicated with them in ways that foster trust and assure them that you are open to their concerns and input.

When a directive is counterintuitive or wrong, followers of a trusted Character-Based Leader will raise a red flag, asking questions and expressing concerns, just as they would in a premortem for a specific project.

It is your responsibility as a Character-Based Leader to address whatever concerns you can and to take the remaining open issues back to the source of the directive.

But once again, when does perseverance become masked by delusion? We've seen that being persistent comes from having a goal

> *"The difference between perseverance and obstinacy is that one comes from a strong will, and the other from a strong won't."*
> *~ Henry Ward Beecher*

and a plan that we believe can succeed. As Character-Based Leaders, we've been in situations before in which we've set goals, built and led teams, and, more than likely, succeeded at reaching the objectives.

There are times in life, however, when obstacles arise along the path to success. An unknown author once stated, "The road to success is dotted with many tempting parking places." So how do we avoid parking along the road to success? Perhaps Henry Ward Beecher explained it best when he said, "The difference between perseverance and obstinacy is that one comes from a strong will, and the other from a strong won't."

The Origins of Perseverance

Perseverance comes from commitment, hard work, patience and endurance tempered by a strong will to succeed; in that specific order in my opinion. We have to start first with being committed to the goal, because without that commitment, the other responses won't follow. For the hierarchical leader, commitment may be nominal; it's what he or she has been told to do and is therefore where this leader's attention will be focused. For the Character-Based Leader, however, commitment comes from a belief that the goal is right, proper and true and that the goal will be of benefit to those affected by it as well as to those who bring the goal to fruition.

When the Character-Based Leader is faced with a directive that is not intrinsically right, proper or true, a wrestling takes place in that leader. At the end of that tussle, the leader will either be able to see the directive in one of those contexts or will have questions or concerns with which to go back to leadership. Either way, you can be sure that with the Character-Based Leader seeking to refine and improve the goal, the results will be significant.

Once the commitment of the Character-Based Leader is secured, hard work naturally follows. This leader seeks to share a vision with his team that communicates the ultimate value of the goal to everyone involved. As people buy in to that goal, progress can start being made.

The problem is that when obstacles appear, it can shake the commitment of the affected team members. They need to see the Character-Based Leader demonstrate the patience and endurance that will ultimately make the goal achievable. When we're able to bear difficulties calmly, without them completely stalling our progress toward a goal, and we're willing to keep trying despite the obstacles, we start to see significant progress that others would have missed because they would simply have given up.

The Role of Passion

If commitment is the key to perseverance, what reinforces commitment? The answer is simple. It's passion. People have no problems with committing their time, money and other resources to something they are passionate about.

Look at examples from history of individuals who have persevered despite seemingly insurmountable odds.

There's the stutterer who went on to become a much-loved actor of both film and stage. As a child of five, his stutter was so severe that he refused to even speak! He remained functionally mute for eight years, until a high school teacher discovered his love for writing poetry and helped him find his way out of his self-imposed silence. He went on to perform in more than 100 films and was nominated for an Academy Award, nine Emmy Awards (three of which he won), five Golden Globe Awards (winning one), an Independent Spirit Award, two Screen Actors Guild Awards (once again, winning one) and three Tony Awards (winning two). And there were other awards as well. You may recognize him as the voice of Darth Vader in the Star Wars series or as Mufasa in *The Lion King.* Or you may know him from *Dr. Strangelove, The Great White Hope, The Hunt for Red October, Patriot Games,* or *The Sandlot,* among many other beloved roles. His name is James Earl Jones.

For Jones, his passion for the power of words and for acting solidified his commitment to his stagecraft and granted him patience when it was needed and endurance to continue pursuing his goals even when they may have seemed unachievable.

So, going back to our earlier question, when does perseverance cross the line and become delusion? An unknown author stated, "The greatest oak was once a little nut who held its ground." It's the same thing with perseverance. As long as there is passion for and commitment to a goal and that passion is matched by the patience and endurance to pursue it, there's no fear of delusion. However, when the passion and commitment are not aligned with the patience and endurance, you run the risk of dropping the pursuit of the goal too early. At that point, all of the time and energy "wasted" in pursuit of the goal was folly and the whole thing becomes delusional.

Think about Thomas Edison and the story of his inventing the first long-lasting light bulb. He made more than 1,000 attempts at his creation, but he didn't view those attempts as failures. Instead, he chose to view them as the learning experiences that brought him closer to a successful invention. They were 1,000 ways *not* to make a light bulb.

It's important to note that the very first light bulb was not invented by Edison, but by Sir Joseph Wilson Swan, who demonstrated the theoretical concept, but gave up trying to develop a practical application after only three attempts. In this example, who would you consider delusional? The man who spawned the idea, but gave up without seeing it come to fruition, or the man who was passionate enough about the possibilities that he didn't give up trying and ultimately succeeded in reaching his goal?

Albert Einstein attributed his persistence and perseverance to the success of his pursuits, stating, "It's not that I'm so smart, it's just that I stay with problems longer." Oftentimes, we're inclined to give up the pursuit of a goal too early because of the fear of being viewed as delusional crackpots. If everything were easy in this world, that would make sense! But we know that many of the greatest accomplishments in this world were not easy things to do. So, if the Character-Based Leader wants to achieve great things in life, why even consider giving up early? *That* is what delusional crackpots do! You're only deluded if you think that something major can be achieved simply by the desire to achieve it. It takes hard work, patience, endurance and lots of perseverance, as things inevitably don't turn out the way you expected.

Newt Gingrich stated that "perseverance is the hard work you do after you get tired of doing the hard work you already did." Swan certainly did not persevere, but Edison did. What's the difference between them? Swan wasn't passionate about his idea. Therefore, he was not committed to seeing it through. It was a nice idea, but nothing more to him. He was shortsighted and missed the potential implications of such an invention. Edison, in contrast, caught the vision, became passionate

> *The greatest oak was once a little nut who held its ground.*

about its pursuit, and was committed to seeing it succeed. This gave him all the patience and endurance he needed to reach his goal.

Developing Self-Mastery

In every instance, developing the characteristic of perseverance requires efforts at self-mastery. Other people cannot make us persevere, although they can encourage us to do so. Perseverance is as much about what's in our hearts and minds as it is about what we do each day. Do we let fears of what others might think keep us from pursuing our passions? Do we withhold our commitment to a project because we might fail?

In martial arts, instructors often share this definition of success with students: Success is getting up one more time than you were knocked down. It's not being perfect. Failure only comes when you refuse to get up again. No one can make you get up again; only your own internal fortitude and resolve can do that, even though others can encourage you and give you a hand up. It's still our determination to persevere that ultimately allows us to claim success.

To accomplish self-mastery, we often have to take our large goals and break them down into smaller, more achievable goals. We must push ourselves to achieve and celebrate each of those goals individually. The collective successes will result in us attaining our large goals as well, with plenty of boosts of our confidence and commitment as steps are made that bring us nearer our desired results. This thought is echoed in a book by Walter Elliott entitled *The Spiritual Life*, which states "Perseverance is not a long race; it is many short races one after another."

Each of these smaller goals will bring you closer to achieving the larger goal, just as a stone cutter hammering away at a rock knows that it was all the earlier blows that ultimately contributed to the rock finally splitting; not just the final blow.

> *"Perseverance is the hard work you do after you get tired of doing the hard work you already did."*
> *~ Newt Gingrich*

Over time, goals will shift and change, yet all the steps made in a specific direction will still assist you in reaching your destination. It's only when you're sitting still and doing nothing that you stay where you already are.

Mules Unite!

As I've grown and matured over the years and developed my Character-Based Leadership skills, I've come to appreciate mules much more than I did before. While they're not as grand or majestic as lions or eagles, they have their place! Without the persistence and endurance that they model, there's so much that would never be achieved. Great discoveries would never be made, enduring contributions to society would be lost, and progress would slow to a trickle.

Chapter 23

Tomorrow's Leaders

Deborah Costello

As a teacher, I attended my 26th high school graduation this year and watched the newest graduates proudly walk across the stage to receive their diplomas. I thought hard about these young people and was struck by how different they were than the students I watched graduate 25 years ago, how different they were than I was when I graduated from high school.

One thing that was not different was the pride their families felt and the feelings of hope and possibility that hung in the air during the ceremony. Each year as I watch students graduate, I am again struck by the feeling of bearing witness to the future, to seeing our doctors and businesspeople, lawyers and authors set sail into the great unknown. What will each become? Will we lose this one to a drug overdose as we did another one earlier this spring? Will I watch that one give a TEDtalk on cracking an international spy ring as I did last fall?

With the prevalence of social media, I "see" graduates far more often, watch them learn and grow in daily diary entries rather than in five-year reunion snapshots. I offer you some of the recent Facebook status updates from a pair of my newly graduated seniors, both significant leaders in their class:

> **Sarah**: *"There is only one you."*
>
> *"Be what you are. This is the first step toward becoming better than you are."*
> *~ Julius Charles Hare*
>
> *"Do what you can with what you have, where you are."*

> **Mike**: *"took a nap and now my bed smells like sunscreen, damn."*
>
> *"Off to bocaaaaa"*
> *"home.food.sleep.aloe."*

Both of these individuals are strong A and B students, both from intact families. Both will attend college. Both were captains of their respective sports teams. They are well-known in our community, well-liked, followed and respected. They are leaders, but I am struck by the differences in their focus. Each of them is equipped with so much potential, so much opportunity. These are the students who could make a difference wherever they end up in life. They have natural intelligence and winning personalities.

These two are a private case study for me, one that may take 20 years to reveal itself completely, and the outcome may say nothing or everything about our culture, our educational system, and our understanding of development. You want to know what happens. I do too, and not just to Sarah and Mike, but to all our children. Is there anything we can do, individually or collectively, to help our kids realize their dreams, lead more effectively than we have done, and become better than we ever were? Is this not a parent's dream? Is it not our society's dream? The answer to all these questions is yes, emphatically yes, yes, yes.

Let's begin with what we know about how humans develop. Neurology has taught us that we are forever making new neurons. Our experiences shape us, and our brains respond by strengthening and increasing the neural connections in frequent experiences. Things we rarely experience have weaker and fewer neural connections. Liken this idea to a forest with many paths. Those we travel often are well-cleared and easy to traverse. Important locations have many paths that lead to them. It is easy to return to such places, and we do so over and over.

Some of our paths are overgrown and difficult to traverse, however. We seldom use them and often get lost. These places are rarely visited and as a result are not well understood.

The reason our understanding of neurology is important is because we and our children are constantly making these connections based on experiences. The interactions that we experience every day clear some paths and allow others to become overgrown. As a species, we are constantly learning and growing, assimilating information and making thousands of decisions. Behaviors, words, and thoughts in our environments are constantly reshaping and changing our brains.

Combine this knowledge with our understanding of moral development. Lawrence Kohlberg outlines three basic stages of moral development and traces human progress through them. First is "preconventional morality." In this stage, we see things as right and wrong based on the likelihood of reward or punishment. We see this decision-making process going on in toddlers and adults, decisions based solely on doing what's best for the individual, be it sneaking a cookie or making an off-the-book stock trade.

"Conventional morality" is the idea that rules and laws are important in a civilized society and that negotiations can be made to enhance everyone's experience. An elementary school trade of my peanut butter sandwich for your bag of grapes is echoed in our adult transactions where I exchange my hard-earned cash for your handcrafted quilt. I could take your quilt, but we have rules against that and I choose not to steal it, not because I will be caught, but because the rules society has created ensure a safe and fair community that we both value.

Finally, Kohlberg describes the rare state of "postconventional morality." In this process, we see actions that are actually beyond the laws created by society. Here, individuals or groups may knowingly disobey a law or rule because the action is more important than the law. We can see this morality in peaceful protests of injustice such as those by Martin Luther King Jr. The behaviors can be disruptive to society and can result in imprisonment, anger, and resistance. Kohlberg states that this final level of morality is seldom seen, as there are few true examples of selfless adherence to higher moral principles regardless of consequences.

Kohlberg goes on to tell us that we are always shifting among these states of morality. Our thousand daily decisions are not confined to one level or another, but are in constant flux due to our own biological and environmental states. The thief today will pay his bill tomorrow; this morning's playground bully is the selfless math tutor at 3 p.m.

Our changing neurology and fluctuating morality are subject to our environment, but this landscape shifts under our feet as well. Even our definitions of ethics, morality, and values change over time. There are no universally defined rules, laws, or standards. Some ethical principles are based on ideas of justice, charity, generosity, respect, and utilitarianism, but the degree to which each of these is important varies widely. A society's laws reflect current acceptable behaviors and views, but these laws do not create our definitions of ethics or morality. Religion has provided guiding principles by which societies can live positively and harmoniously, but religious diversity precludes universal acceptance of any given set of principles. We need only glance at our history and current events to know that no matter how noble our intentions or passionate our adherence, religion has not provided a consistent and widely accepted set of ethics and values. In essence, ethics are an ever-changing reflection of and influence on ourselves and others.

Since we are ever-changing and the environment is as well, everything matters. Every experience is an input in the development of the changing ethics of our community and in the changing neurology of our minds. Thousands of hours of television and video games combine with thousands of hours spent in school and at work, playing sports, doing community service, and chatting online with friends. Vacations matter. Family dinner matters. Fights matter. A poorly chosen word when you're tired, a hug at the right moment, the way you enforce rules, upholding your standards, tolerating bad behavior, forgetting to apologize; it all matters. And not just to your own kids. Everywhere you go, someone sees you and learns from you, and the fabric of our society's ethics and the complex landscape of our own brains are created every minute, stitch by stitch, path by path, by every person's behavior. It all matters. Everything we do, think, and feel matters.

Are you afraid yet? Sometimes I am. If everything and everyone matters, it seems hopeless. There's so much bad in the world, there are so many examples of anger and pain, violence and evil and selfishness, that it seems overwhelming. If you really care about the future of our society and the environment we are creating for our kids, then all this seems pretty scary. Humans are inherently flawed. We make mistakes every single day. Everyone does. Our children see this, our colleagues and friends see this; in fact, everyone sees others make mistakes. As humans, it is important that we care deeply about leadership and role-modeling, and everything that adulthood can stand for. Most importantly, we must experience the thousands of human decisions around us and decide what we ourselves will do in our own decision-making processes. That is why it is so important that our children see us, see everyone, make mistakes. We not only need to learn how to do what's right, but we also need to learn how to fix what we do wrong.

In the end, we do not need to be afraid. We all matter. We all make mistakes. We all fix them. We all try again. That's what you're teaching your children, your neighbors, the guy behind you in the Starbucks line, and yourself. This is how you lead, and like it or not, you are a leader. In every decision you make, every action you take, you are a leader, and how you lead matters.

Consider my student Sarah. She's only 18, but she's already rearranging my neurons, affecting my environment, showing me and her 1,000 Facebook friends that everyone matters. She is already doing exactly what we all need to do as best we can. Remember what Sarah told all her Facebook friends and go forward boldly, confidently, and with purpose.

"Do what you can with what you have, where you are."
~ Theodore Roosevelt

Questions to Ponder on Becoming a Character-Based Leader

Chery Gegelman

Character-Based Leadership is the conscious choice to be an ambassador, to place the greater good, the purpose of the organization, and the needs of others above your own desires. It requires a choice to lead with integrity, and the understanding that everything you do is observed and evaluated by others as either authentic or disingenuous.

- How do you greet people when you see them?
- How do you treat people when you are under pressure?
- Do you follow through on your commitments?
- What do you say about others when they are not around?
- Are your actions and directions to others ethical?

Character-Based Leadership means walking around and engaging with others, asking questions, and seeking first to understand.

- Are there specific concerns? Have these concerns been addressed?
- Is the direction clear?
- Are the necessary tools available?
- Is consistent support provided?

Character-Based Leadership means having the courage to consistently speak truth instead of giving in to fear and politics.

- What are the specific items that are creating barriers to success or that are increasing risk?
- Does anyone else need to be involved?
- What are you doing to make sure the obstacles are being removed?

Finally, Character-Based Leadership requires balancing both compassion and accountability for your own actions and in addressing the actions of others.

- What have you learned about root causes for this issue?
    - What have you done or not done to contribute to this issue?
    - How can you take ownership of this issue?
- Are historical patterns being repeated with the expectation of different results?
    - Are there signs of improvement, or are you managing decline?
    - Is it time to change strategies?

A... leader is an individual who blends extreme personal humility with intense professional will. ~ ***Jim Collins***

About the Authors

Tara Alemany

Owner, Aleweb Social Marketing

Board of Directors, Forest Haven, Inc.

Tara R. Alemany is the owner and founder of Aleweb Social Marketing. (In keeping with the times, her teenaged daughter created the "Aleweb" name as a mash-up between their last name and "the web.") Tara brings more than 20 years of experience writing, training, and providing application support and business process analysis. All of these skills are used in helping her clients achieve their goals. She is frequently recognized for her speaking ability, knowledge and expertise, which she leverages to educate technophobes and trendsetters in a variety of age groups.

Tara has her own blog, "The Conversations Around Us," but also guest blogs, writes for the Lead Change Group, has written for SmartBrief and Carol Roth's Business Unplugged, and has had her work reprinted in *SOLD* magazine. She has published an eBook (*The Plan that Launched a Thousand Books*) as well, and is working on her next book, *The Best is Yet to Come*.

She speaks frequently on social media topics, and has been a speaker or panelist at local events as well as at larger conferences, including the eMarketing Association's "The Power of eMarketing" conference, SMCampLI (a social media conference in Long Island), and a chapter meeting of the International Association of Microsoft Channel Partners.

About the Authors

She is also a motivational speaker, sharing thoughts and ideas learned from personal experience on becoming a winner of Life's challenges.

In addition to providing consulting services, writing and speaking, Tara serves on the Board of Directors of a nonprofit ministry, is chaplain of her local Word Weavers chapter, and is also a martial artist, a short-term missionary, a musician, and a homeschooling mom to two kids (one of each), ages 14 and 12.

Connect with Tara online -

Website/Blog: alewebsocial.com | **Facebook:** facebook.com/AlewebSocial | **Twitter:** @eandtsmom | **LinkedIn:** linkedin.com/in/taraalemany | **Google+:** gplus.to/taraalemany | **E-mail:** tara@alewebsocial.com

Chad Balthrop

Minister of Leadership Development, Owasso's First Baptist Church

Chad Balthrop is a husband, father and Minister of Leadership Development at Owasso's First Baptist Church. He is a teaching pastor whose creative work challenges and equips people to answer the question "What's next in my spiritual journey?" He is a producer for the Oklahoma Youth Evangelism Conference and has served as the media director for Falls Creek Baptist Assembly, the largest youth camp in the nation. He loves a good story and would love to hear yours!

Connect with Chad online -

Blog: www.thefarpoint.org | **Facebook**: facebook.com/ChadBalthrop | **Twitter**: @ChadBalthrop

Meghan M. Biro

Founder, TalentCulture

Meghan M. Biro is a globally recognized leader in talent strategy and a pioneer in building the business case for brand humanization. Founder of TalentCulture and a serial entrepreneur, Meghan creates successful ventures by navigating the complexities of career and workplace branding.

In her practice as a social recruiter and strategist, Meghan has placed hundreds of individuals with clients ranging from Fortune 500s to the most innovative software start-up companies in the world, including Google, Microsoft and emerging companies in the social technology and media marketplace.

She is also an accomplished consultant who has helped hundreds of individuals from all levels in the organization (C level executives, mid-career, mid-level managers, software architects and recent college graduates) and across generations (Gen Y to baby boomers) develop effective career strategies that propel them to achieve personal and professional success.

Meghan is a blogger on the subjects of leadership, recruiting, workforce culture, personal and corporate branding, and social media in HR. She is founder and co-host of the Twitter chat "#TChat, The World of Work," a long-standing weekly chat and radio show, and the co-host of #HRTechChat, a community dedicated to addressing the business needs of the rapidly evolving people-technology landscape.

Meghan's thoughts and ideas are often quoted on top publications such as Forbes, CBS Moneywatch, Glassdoor, Monster, and the HR, social media and leadership hub of your choice.

About the Authors

Connect with Meghan online -

Website: www.talentculture.com | **Facebook:** facebook.com/MeghanMBiro | **Twitter:** @MeghanMBiro | **LinkedIn:** linkedin.com/in/meghanmbiro

S. Max Brown

Vice President, Leadership Initiatives, Rideau Recognition Solutions

In the past ten years, **Max Brown** has made more than 1,000 presentations in locations all around the world. He's taken clients rappelling off the Great Wall of China, facilitated at the Parliament of World Religions Conference in Spain, and spoken in hundreds of cities including Athens, Beijing, Hong Kong, Mumbai, Paris, New York, Vancouver, and Sydney… Nebraska.

With his experience in leadership training, speaking, and facilitating around the world, Max brings a global perspective to the challenge of motivating people. Audiences at organizations such as American Express, GE, HSBC, The Nature Conservancy, and the Canadian federal government have raved about his interactive, engaging style. As a result, he travels 200,000 miles per year to deliver presentations to clients around the world!

Max laces his presentations with stories and examples that inspire people to act. He is consistently given high ratings, including an "all-star" recommended speaker designation from the International Association of Business Communicators. Max has a certificate in leadership coaching from Georgetown University and a master's degree in organizational learning from George Mason University, and he is a member of the National Speaker's Association.

Connect with Max online -

Blog: Rideau.com | **Weekly Radio:** RealRecognitionRadio.com | **Twitter:** @SMaxBrown

Page Cole

Owner, Visiting Angels of Green Country

Page Cole has been developing leaders for more than 30 years as a pastor, with his last role as executive pastor of First Baptist Church, Owasso. He now owns Visiting Angels of Green Country, a non-medical home health company. His passion continues to be in mentoring young leaders. He's husband to Ronda and dad to Erin, Nathan, and Ben.

Connect with Page online -

Website: www.visitingangels.com/greencountry | **Blog:** www.rhinofordinner.com | **Facebook:** facebook.com/page.cole | **Twitter:** @pagecole | **LinkedIn:** linkedin.com/in/pagecole

Heather Coleman-Voss

Career and Social Media Coach, Corporate Trainer and Speaker

Heather Coleman-Voss is a passionate speaker on the topics of social media marketing and management, personal branding, career strategies and leadership. She is a contributing author to the Lead Change Group and Hire Friday, a radio guest, and a guest blogger on several career and leadership sites.

Heather is a social media, career and leadership consultant, and a corporate trainer and speaker with the Mythic Group, LLC.

Proud to instruct upcoming graduates and those in career transition, Heather Coleman-Voss is the Social Media Manager of Career Services and an instructor at Specs Howard School of Media Arts. Heather is excited to work for a school so focused on developing the specialized talents of each student while supporting them in their future careers.

Heather is happily married to Paul Voss, and the couple blended their family in November 2010. Together, they have three children and a busy, though quite a wonderful, life.

Connect with Heather online -

Facebook: facebook.com/heatherecoleman | **Twitter:** @HeatherEColeman | **LinkedIn:** linkedin.com/in/HeatherEColeman | **Google+:** gplus.to/heatherecoleman

Deborah Costello

Teacher

Deborah Costello has been a teacher of high school mathematics, psychology, and leadership for more than 20 years. She currently serves as Mathematics Department Chair at a small private school in Orlando, Florida. In the past decade, she has worked with colleagues to improve school-wide professional development, increase technology integration, and effectively harness social media. She has coached Quiz Bowl, swimming, softball, volleyball, and bowling.

Deb also serves as a consultant for the College Board, traveling throughout the United States to train beginning AP calculus teachers, and has been an AP calculus reader for the past six years. Recently, she has been an occasional blogger for the Lead Change Group. Her current passions include fundraising for breast cancer research and coaching women triathletes.

Deb is married and raising two rowdy teenage boys and her rambunctious black lab, Lucy.

Connect with Deb online -

Twitter: @costelloland | **LinkedIn:** linkedin.com/pub/deb-costello/7/965/3a1 | **Triathlon Team Website:** http://swim-bike-run-repeat.blogspot.com/

Mónica Diaz

Director, Quidam Global

Mónica Diaz lives in Mexico and works around the globe to help companies and individuals create and maintain healthy corporate cultures. She has been a leader in different capacities for most of her life and a facilitator of the Human Element® approach since 1987.

Her background in higher education and human potential and her boundless enthusiasm make her an engaging speaker, author and coach with a unique style of delivery and provocative thinking.

In 2010, she attended the LeaderPalooza Unconference, becoming one of the initial instigators for Lead Change.

Her coaching model has helped coaches around the world assist their clients in building increased capacity for action that is measurable by self, organization and others. She has published innumerable articles and blog posts over the years. Her book, *Otheresteem, Regaining the Power to Value Others* takes a practical approach to valuing people consistently for increased self-esteem and sense of community.

Her current work includes Aspirations Theory, which she is deepening in collaboration with Randall Krause, and two books in the making. She is a passionate advocate of human connection through social media and is currently active in several online ventures to make her point. She is very proud to be a part of this book!

Connect with Mónica online -

Book: www.otheresteem.org | **Blog:** www.e-quidam.com/theblog | **Twitter:** @monedays | **LinkedIn:** mx.linkedin.com/in/monicadiazdeperalta | **More Info:** www.thehumanelement.com

Sonia DiMaulo

Founder, Harvest Performance

At Harvest Performance, we use the power of authentic feedback to cultivate *trust and collaboration.* How do you cultivate trust and collaboration to positively affect your team?

Sonia Di Maulo (BA, MA) is a founder, feedback enthusiast, speaker, leader, performance-improvement professional, and creator of award-winning programs. She is passionate about helping leaders find the right performance strategies to grow their teams' potential for trust and collaboration. Her proven 3+1 feedback strategy harvests connection and boosts individual and team performances.

Sonia has published articles in *PerformanceXpress* and *Human Resources IQ.* She is also a contributor of the Lead Change Group (a global leadership community of leaders growing leaders) and of In the Loop (a guide to getting the most out of work).

She launched her first book in April 2012, *The Apple in the Orchard: a story about finding the courage to emerge as a leader*. The Apple's journey provides a glimpse into the power of living systems as models for sustainability, collaboration, and growth.

She is currently working on her new book *Expose Exceptional Performance*, a guide to successful implementation of her 3+1 feedback strategy.

Connect with Sonia online -

Facebook: www.facebook.com/theappleintheorchard | **Twitter:** @readytofeedback | **Linkedin:** ca.linkedin.com/in/soniadimaulo | **E-mail:** sonia@harvestperformance.ca

Georgia Feiste

President, Collaborative Transitions Coaching, Inc.

Georgia Feiste specializes in leadership and personal growth and training. Her focus is on helping women executives and leaders grow their character-based leadership and collaboration skills in their career, business, and personal lives. Georgia has more than 30 years of executive leadership experience in corporations, nonprofits, and her community. She has served on multiple boards in a variety of officer positions. Georgia believes that character is the underlying foundation to true leadership, and she teaches about these concepts in her transformational leadership programs and workshops.

Connect with Georgia online -

Website/Blog: collaborativetransitions.com | **Facebook:** facebook.com/collaborativetransitionscoachng | **Twitter:** @feistycoach | **LinkedIn:** linkedin.com/in/georgiafeiste | **Google+:** gplus.to/georgiafeiste | **E-mail:** Georgia@CollaborativeTransitions.com

Chery Gegelman

President and Managing Partner, Giana Consulting, LLC

Chery Gegelman is a visionary, a nurturing and energetic presence who has been described by others as honest, courageous and dedicated. She has been gifted with an ability to understand the strengths and opportunities of both individuals and organizations. Through a unique blend of almost childlike curiosity, creativity and deeply rooted strength, she helps clients resolve issues and discover new paths.

Chery is the president of Giana Consulting, an organizational wholeness and growth consulting company, and specializes in organizational development, leadership and change. Chery is available for consulting, facilitating, speaking and collaborating.

She is quick to point out that any wisdom and understanding she brings come from her own failures and successes, and the people she worked with along the way: wise mentors, years of study and the undeserved grace of her Heavenly Father.

Connect with Chery online -

Website: www.gianaconsulting.com | **Blog:** www.gianaconsulting.com/blog.php | **Facebook:** facebook.com/GianaConsulting | **Twitter:** @GianaConsulting | **LinkedIn:** linkedin.com/in/gianaconsulting | **Google+:** gplus.to/GianaConsulting | **YouTube:** youtube.com/user/CheryGegelman | **BlogNotions:** leadership.blognotions.com/cgegelman/ | **E-mail:** cgegelman@gianaconsulting.com

Christina Haxton

Founder and President, Sustainable Leadership, Inc.

Christina Haxton offers a unique combination of professional experience, training and education in the psychology of interpersonal communication, the brain science behind motivation and humor, with more than 20 years of experience in business. As the founder and president of Sustainable Leadership, Inc., Christina assists newly promoted senior managers and recently hired executive-level leaders to discover advanced tools to quickly build trust with their new teams. Christina's clients learn how to discover their strengths to solve challenging problems, making them exceptionally successful at what they do. Christina has a degree in psychology from UCLA, a master's degree in marriage & family counseling from Phillips Graduate Institute, and an evidence-based coaching certificate from Fielding Graduate University. As a business owner (times two) and serial entrepreneur for more than 15 years and a wife and mother of two fabulous children, in her free time, Christina enjoys competing in reining horse shows in Colorado with her horse, Deuce.

Connect with Christina online -

Website: sustainable-leaders.com | **Twitter:** @ChristinaHaxton | **LinkedIn:** linkedin.com/in/christinahaxton | **E-mail:** christina@sustainable-leaders.com

Mike Henry Sr.

Chief Instigator, Lead Change Group

Mike Henry is the founder and Chief Instigator of the Lead Change Group, a global community of leadership-development professionals dedicated to instigating a leadership revolution by applying Character-Based Leadership to make a positive difference.

He's an initiator and a catalyst, connecting people and mobilizing change.

Mike is also a leadership-development specialist and consultant who helps leaders at all levels gain perspective and accept responsibility for their jobs and for the big picture of the organization. He speaks, consults and coaches individuals and groups to lead through relationships regardless of their positions or power in organizations. Mike loves to mobilize and energize leaders to overcome obstacles and deepen their characters as the foundation for their leadership.

Mike also enjoys connecting people through social media or face-to-face.

Connect with Mike online -

Website: leadchangegroup.com | **Twitter:** @mikehenrysr | **LinkedIn:** linkedin.com/in/mikehenrysr

Will Lukang

PMP, CSM, CLDC

Will Lukang seeks every opportunity to learn and grow so that he is able to pass his knowledge to younger generations. He is passionate about people and leadership development, coaching and mentoring. He always looks at the positive side of every situation.

Will's leadership journey started in 2001, when he attended Seton Hall University's Master of Arts in Strategic Communication and Leadership (MASCL) program, where he graduated with honors. He is a public speaker on leadership. He presented at the Learning Leaders Symposium in Fort Myers, Florida, on "Developing Talent Around Us, Strengthening Relationships One at a Time." Aside from pursuing his passion for leadership and talent development, Will is a certified project manager from PMI and a Certified Scrum Master.

Will has more than 21 years of experience in the information technology industry. He holds an MBA in information decision and technology management from IONA College, where he also graduated with honors, and a BS in commerce (majoring in accounting) from the University of Santo Tomas.

In his free time, he loves to read books, blog and play golf with his daughter. He also enjoys spending time with his lovely wife and two adorable daughters.

Connect with Will online -

Blog: willlukang.wordpress.com | **Twitter:** @will_lukang

About the Authors

Susan Mazza

Managing Partner and President, Clarus Consulting Group, LLC

Susan works with individuals and organizations to develop leaders, and support them in cultivating relationships that work and delivering results that matter. A certified leadership coach, motivational speaker, professional facilitator and business consultant she is known for bringing clarity to thinking, transforming theory and ideas into effective action, and instigating leadership at all levels.

Based on over 25 years of experience working with diverse people and organizations from around the world, Susan developed The Art of Accountability™. This methodology empowers individuals and organizations to build more trusting relationships, develop personal leadership skills, and instill the practices and culture of accountability.

Believing that you don't have to be the leader to be a leader Susan speaks and writes about the simple yet powerful acts of everyday leadership: Speaking Up, Stepping Up, Standing Up™. The author of the Random Acts of Leadership™ blog, she is also a contributing blogger for the Lead Change Group and Talent Culture communities and was among the founding instigators in the Lead Change Group.

Susan graduated from the Pennsylvania State University with a BS in finance and international business. She lives in Vero Beach, Florida, with her husband, daughter and two dogs.

Connect with Susan online -

Website/Blog: www.RandomActsofLeadership.com | **Twitter:** @SusanMazza | **LinkedIn:** linkedin.com/in/SusanMazza | **E-mail:** Susan@RandomActsofLeadership.com

Jennifer Miller

Managing Partner, SkillSource

Since the age of seven, when she became a big sister for the first time, **Jennifer V. Miller** has been living a life of Character-Based Leadership. She's crafted a career abundant with leadership stories: manager for three Fortune 500 companies, project team leader, mentor and board member. As the first female president of the Grand Rapids Networking Group and the youngest member of the executive committee for the Junior Achievement/Great Lakes division, Jennifer's leadership journey has broken barriers and given her insight into how to ethically navigate the often murky waters of organizational politics.

Jennifer is the managing partner of SkillSource, a niche consultancy that helps emerging leaders master the people equation. Jennifer combines her education in behavioral psychology with her experience as a human resources generalist and training facilitator to develop the people skills of those who want to maximize their influence and professionalism. Her writing has appeared in college textbooks, magazines and major media outlets such as Forbes.com.

Connect with Jennifer online -

Blog: people-equation.com | **Twitter:** @jennifervmiller | **Facebook:** facebook.com/SkillSource

Jane Perdue

Principal and CEO, Braithwaite Innovation Group
Co-Founder, Get Your Big On

"If you put your heart and mind to it, you can do anything a man can do – and do it even better." Inspired by these words from her Dad, Jane Perdue set out to tackle Corporate America. She worked as a vice president for 15 years at Fortune 100 telecommunications companies, including Comcast and AT&T Broadband. Often the only female executive at the table, Jane put her MBA to good use there, managing $25 million budgets and thousands of employees, creating and executing strategy, negotiating labor contracts, developing leaders, mentoring women, and accumulating a stunning collection of purses.

Beginning to think her dad might have had it wrong, Jane left Corporate America after a boss described her as "Aunt Polly" and founded Braithwaite Innovation Group, a female-owned, professional development firm. In her second act of life, Jane works as a leadership and women's issues expert, speaker and author. She is on the Board of Directors for the Charleston, SC Center for Women, the largest women's development center in the state, and created and manages their new Women's Leadership Institute.

Jane is the author of *Yes You Can!*, a leadership anthology co-authored with Warren Bennis, and writes for the *Post and Courier* newspaper. Her articles have appeared in SmartBrief, Insights, Forbes and The Glass Hammer.

A former Women in Cable Telecommunications Board Member, WICT Mentor of the Year, Betsy Magness Leadership Institute alumna and certified polarity consultant, Jane has appeared as an expert on leadership and women in business topics in newspapers, magazines, radio, and television. She has presented at numerous conferences including the Society of Human Resource Management, the Women in

Business Conference, ThinkTEC Innovation Summit, and Women in Cable Telecommunications.

Connect with Jane online -

Websites: www.braithwaiteinnovationgroup *and* getyourbigon.com |
Twitter: @thehrgoddess | **LinkedIn:** linkedin.com/in/janeperdue | **Blog:**
getyourbigon.com/leadbigblog/

Lisa Petrilli

CEO, C-Level Strategies, Inc.
COO and CMO, To Be a Woman Global Platform
CRO (Chief Relationship Officer), CEO Connection

Lisa Petrilli's corporate leadership experience includes running a $750 million medication delivery business and a team of marketers while negotiating global licensing, commercialization and co-marketing contracts with pharma-ceutical companies. She also spent a year as a corporate executive leadership trainer.

Early in her career when faced with a PR challenge by Greenpeace, she led a team that created a solution so unique and environmentally friendly that she presented it on behalf of her company to a United Nations environmental conference in Geneva, Switzerland.

Lisa has an MBA from Northwestern University's Kellogg Graduate School of Management in marketing, international business and organizational behavior and a bachelor's degree from Indiana University's Honor's College and Kelley School of Business with a minor in political science.

Lisa is author of the eBook *The Introvert's Guide to Success in Business and Leadership*. She is also a Harvard Business Review blogger, and was featured in the 10th Anniversary Edition of *The Power of Focus* by Jack Canfield, Mark Victor Hansen and Les Hewitt. She is author of Visionary Leadership Blog; is a contributing blogger for the Lead Change Group; is co-founder and co-host of "Leadership Chat" on Twitter, garnering millions of online impressions each week; and was named one of Twitter's Small-Business Big Shots in the Wall Street Journal.

Connect with Lisa online -

Blog: www.lisapetrilli.com | **Twitter:** @ lisapetrilli | **LinkedIn:** linkedin.com/in/lisapetrilli | **Google+:** gplus.to/lisapetrilli | **E-mail:** Lisa@CLevelStrategies.com

Dan Rockwell

Blogger, Leadership Freak

Dan Rockwell believes we are what we were when we were in our early teens. That makes him a farm boy from Maine, even though he's been in central Pennsylvania for 25 years. He's been leading for all his life and has broad experiences in the education, governmental, corporate, and not-for-profit arenas.

Currently, he gives corporate, community, and church presentations; delivers leadership and management training; and coaches emerging leaders.

Although Dan's best known for leadership, social media is his secret passion. He loves connecting with people who follow his active Twitter and Facebook accounts.

In addition to writing the Leadership Freak blog, Dan writes for the American Management Association, the Society for Human Resource Management, the Deloitte Leadership Academy, and others.

Connect with Dan online -

Blog: leadershipfreak.wordpress.com | **Facebook:** facebook.com/LeadershipFreak | **Twitter:** @leadershipfreak | **E-mail:** dan@leadershipfreak.com

Mary Schaefer

President and Lead Consultant, Artemis Path, Inc

As a speaker, coach, trainer and HR professional, **Mary Schaefer** has more than 25 years of experience working with organizations to create manager-employee communication breakthroughs and positive functional work cultures.

Mary C. Schaefer has 20 years of experience as a corporate employee for a Fortune 100 company, her last role being an HR manager with a constituency of more than 550 people. She began her own leadership development growing up on a melon farm in Southern Indiana.

Mary's clients range from Fortune 500 companies to local nonprofits and small businesses. She has served in a variety of roles in chemical plant, office, IT and lab environments.

She has taught HR topics at both Delaware Technical & Community College and Wilmington University. Mary's clients include Xerox, Siemens, DuPont and Ahold USA.

Mary has published online on the sites of organizations such as Toolbox for HR, Today's Financial Woman, National Association of Female Executives, and of course, the Lead Change Group.

Mary's passion is transforming organizations so they unleash the power and potential of human beings treating each other humanly at work.

Connect with Mary online -

Website: www.ReImagineWork.com | **Twitter:** @MarySchaefer | **LinkedIn:** linkedin.com/in/maryschaefer

Don Shapiro

President, First Concepts Consultants, Inc.

Don Shapiro is president and founder of First Concepts Consultants, Inc., a sales, marketing and management consulting practice that since 1985 has helped firms in 30 industries to increase their rate of growth and market share. As a Revenue Detective, he investigates ways for firms to increase their sales, margins and market share.

A curious nature, a passion for uncovering what causes things to happen, and a creative spirit have led Don to make many discoveries about why people buy and how they figure out value. After seeing too many of his clients stumble at implementation, Don started focusing on how organizations implement change and improvements. It became clear that everything that happens starts with people, and that requires great leadership.

For more than 30 years, Don has been helping people learn, laugh and leave inspired through his speeches, workshops and training programs. He has had his work published in several magazines and writes three blogs on business and personal issues. Don is a graduate of the Executive Development Program at the UCLA Anderson School of Management.

Connect with Don online -

Website: www.firstconcepts.com | **Facebook:** facebook.com/lifeisaforkintheroad | **Twitter:** @donshapiro1 | **LinkedIn:** linkedin.com/in/donshapiro | **E-mail:** donshapiro@firstconcepts.com

About the Lead Change Group

This book has been written as a community effort by the Lead Change Group, which is a global community dedicated to instigating a leadership revolution.

To us, this means bringing out the best in you and helping you step up and step out as a leader because of who you are. Leaders influence others. Your character determines your influence, whether or not someone "puts you in charge," so this community is a place where you can develop and try out your ideas and skills as you engage the world.

Vision

The Lead Change Group is a not-for-profit, global community dedicated to instigating a leadership revolution.

Mission

We will encourage, energize, and equip one another to apply Character-Based Leadership to *Lead Change*

- in ourselves;
- in others; and
- in our communities.

Our goal is to help each other be producers rather than consumers. We want to be the change.

> To learn more or to become a member, find us online at http://leadchangegroup.com, and be sure to check out our blog, where you'll find great leadership topics to support and encourage you!

Index

Index

Index

CPSIA information can be obtained at www.ICGtesting.com
Printed in the USA
LVOW12s2054301113

363370LV00021B/1882/P